The Haunted Forts and Battlefields of 1812

by C.T. Shooting Star

Illustrations by Susan Hilson

Wells Hamilton Literary Consultants LLC

The Haunted Forts and Battlefields of 1812

by C.T. Shooting Star

Illustrations by Susan Hilson

Wells Hamilton Literary Consultants LLC

The Haunted Forts and Battlefields of 1812

Paperback: (979-8-950072-12-3)

Hardcover: (979-8-950072-13-0)

Wells Hamilton Literary Consultants LLC books may be ordered through booksellers or by contacting:

Wells Hamiton

800 N King St, Wilmington, DE 19801, United States

www.wellshamilton.com

Part One

Haunted Forts and Battlefields

Background

The hatred didn't exist at the beginning of the war. But soon after the Battle of Queenston Heights and the death of General Brock, the War of 1812 became more a case of "survival of the fittest." Besides the brutal fighting, perhaps the most notable aspect of the War of 1812 was the hatred. If not, then why would the dead remain restless?

It was a barbaric war in an inhospitable climate. There were nasty endings from bayonets, swords, musket balls and cannonballs; plus, two huge explosions at Fort York and Fort Erie which resulted in missing bones and unmarked graves.

If you add savagery and death by tomahawk to the following, then death from drowning, freezing, disease, burning and sickness would include a greater number of victims than the major battles.

If you thought that being wounded was a better fate, then think again. Instead of a proper painkiller, the wounded were given rum and a musket ball to clamp between their teeth while they braved the most hideous fate possible for wounded soldiers: the barbaric battlefield medical practice of amputation. If your last memories on earth were "being wounded" before you died, then that agony might also survive the grave.

Because both America and Britain were not prepared to wage war against each other, there was a shortage of regular soldiers to command in 1812. Therefore, the North American armies were also comprised of militia, Native

Americans and part-time soldiers. Moreover, what started as a political row in the seats of power became more of a personal matter at the local level. In addition to the mounting anger, there was pressure on both sides to increase the number of regular troops in the field as the war continued. The increase in regular troops contributed to a more bitter and violent war, with the final result being several large scale battles and a siege.

Why did the dead remain restless? Why indeed.

Introduction

The Niagara area was destined to become the most blood-soaked region within Upper Canada during the War of 1812. More than likely, it will remain the most haunted area in Canada forevermore.

There are many theories about why there are ghosts. They range from the theories of psychic impressions or imprints to the theory of earthbound spirits. According to some of the parapsychology research in the United States, a majority of ghostly visions are replays of the past. The imprints are created because a tragedy or suffering has taken place. An area itself can become sensitized as a result of emotional conflicts involving bloodshed. The sights and sounds of the haunting may be experienced by a sensitive person, as if it were a motion picture being fed through a projector.

Research in England also supports the theory of psychic impressions. Essex contains more than its share of haunted sites and ghostly sightings and is where many bloody conflicts took place. According to expertise in the field, certain soils absorb cosmic waves more readily than others. Soils such as clay, chalk and alluvial soils could be more sensitive to imprinting phenomena than the ancient rocks. A wide variety of research has also pointed out how subterranean water attracts ghostly phenomena. Perhaps there is a similar reason here.

Nevertheless, some ghostly encounters with the past may not be imprints. One well known encounter with spirits from the past was recorded in a book suitably called "An Adventure," written in 1911. According to this fascinating account, the two women who wrote the story visited the court of Marie Antoinette. They became actors in the film at the time of the French Revolution, rather than just passive viewers. Some might say "An Adventure" was more science fiction than time travel. On the other hand, both women were psychically sensitive and were reluctant to come forward with their story.

Earthbound spirits are the last category of ghostly phenomena. In rare cases, an unexpected proper manifestation can develop. Perhaps it is because manifestations are so rare or not reported that many people are skeptical about the existence of ghosts.

The old forts and battlegrounds in the Niagara region of Ontario provide a rich context in which to test various theories of ghostly phenomena. The haunted triangle of Niagara includes Fort George, Fort Niagara and Fort Mississauga. Fort Erie is of interest to the ghost hunter as well because many soldiers died there under appalling conditions. In addition to a huge explosion that claimed the lives of hundreds, Fort Erie was involved in a prolonged siege during the War of 1812. Ghost hunters should also note that there were three major battles fought in the Niagara area. Chippewa, Lundy's Lane and Queenston Heights have all left their psychic residue on the land.

* * *

Newark or Niagara-on-the-Lake, as it is called today, is where Fort George stands. Niagara-on-the-Lake is possibly the most haunted place in Canada on a per capita basis. The reason for its "most haunted" reputation is related to one fateful day, when the entire town was turned into a battlefield.

On May 27, 1813, all fortified British defensive positions in Newark were destroyed by cannon fire from American warships. There were British regulars who stood their ground, but they were vastly outnumbered by the American soldiers during the attack. Newark became blood-soaked from the brutal fighting that took place on that day. Hundreds of soldiers lost their lives within a few hours. The dead soldiers were buried where they fell, in places where people living today might not expect to find graves or the weapons of war.

When the American soldiers left several months later, they set fire to the entire town of Newark. The citizens were forced onto the snow-covered streets, with barely enough to wear. Some stood in their bare feet on whatever household items they could find in order to keep their feet from freezing. Those who were unable to walk had their beds taken out onto the street. Then, the whole town was torched and destroyed.

In regards to bitter ghosts, the best was for the last. Slow freezing was one thing, but the situation for a wounded soldier back then was grim. If you took a musket ball in the arm or leg, it meant automatic amputation. Sometimes the knife or saw wasn't sharp enough or fast enough during a battle; so they just broke the bone instead. The arteries and veins were seared with a very hot object to stem the bleeding. If you were lucky enough to pass out, you would not have to watch your arm or leg being sewn up like a sausage.

Further proof of this expedient method of battlefield medicine was found at Fort Erie. The Americans captured Fort Erie during the War of 1812; but found themselves under siege for several months, before they were finally able to abandon the fort and return home. When they dug up the graves in a fort burial site, over one hundred years later, they found all kinds of broken arms and leg bones, separated from the rest of their skeleton bodies. The spirits who departed under those grisly circumstances would at the very least leave a rather appalling psychic imprint.

All of this evidence suggests that the predominant psychic sensation, gathered from most ghostly activity within the forts and on the battlefields of Niagara, would be that of anger, suffering or sadness. Accordingly, psychics have been known to turn around and walk away from the prevailing negativity in parts of Fort George. Some people have become sick to their stomachs, not once but twice, after recovering and then ignoring these spine-chilling warnings.

The Haunted Forts and Battlefields of Niagara

(August 2004 – July 2006)

Fort Erie

August 2004

The nighttime re-enactment at Fort Erie involves more than just battles. The re-enactors like to give you a realistic taste of military life under stressful conditions. Here is what's going on tonight: there's an amputation being performed on a soldier; there's a bargaining session between an American and British officer; there's a lively interaction between captured British soldiers and an American guard; there's another American soldier who is guarding the fort's ramparts and patrolling in search of the enemy; and finally, there's a treat for all the visitors to the fort who find their way to the kitchen.

But what about the phantoms who reside at the fort?

With all of the action going on at the fort during the evening hours, we decided to look for ghosts during the daytime. The summer students who are employed as staff won't normally tell you about the ghost of the British Captain who lives upstairs and doesn't like his bed made up. One of the bravest soldiers at that fort would not go up to the haunted room because the ghostly Captain kept throwing the bedclothes off "his" bed after it was made up. The young re-enactor soldier finally gave the bed-making job to a female staffer who apologized to the Captain and appealed to him for his co-operation in keeping the place fit for the tourists. It worked. The ghost began to co-operate. Perhaps, some of the ghosts at the fort are friendly after all, if you show respect towards them.

Ghost Tours at Fort George

Summer of 2004

Kyle Upton started the ghost tour at Fort George several years ago. He collected some fascinating ghost stories and wrote a book about them called "The Ghosts of Niagara."

Fort George ghost tour guides are very good as entertainers. Nevertheless, some of the tour guides know more than what they will admit. I connected well with Mark who had been at the fort for 25 years; but his accomplices closed ranks on me and decided to disrupt my attempt to engage with him. I thought that I was only getting started, but my wife Cathy said I was getting too close to the bone and that his back-up crew were being very protective of their prize tour guide. I can honestly say that I don't blame them one bit. At least some of the tour operators know that behind the facade of the ghost tours, there are some very bad psychic spots at the fort.

In the past, the ghost tour guides at Fort George often warned their guests about the "Watcher." So with the following preamble, I've added their warning that was intended to give skeptics the creeps.

Historical Fort George is located near the mouth of the Niagara River and Lake Ontario and you could say that there are a few evil spirits there. There is at least one nasty ghost at the fort called the "Watcher." His face is so evil looking, it can give you nightmares.

One of the fort's staff saw him after he challenged the ghost to appear. Unfortunately, the ghost did appear, in all its glory, just for the staffer. The staffer left his job and packed off as quickly as possible, with a word of warning for the rest of us. The word is this. Don't challenge the ghosts at the fort, especially the Watcher. He is truly horrifying to gaze upon.

Bunkhouse One

Kyle might be entertaining, but Mark had a reputation as being the most successful ghost tour guide at Fort George. He can deliver more ghosts than anyone else. We never doubted his reputation. After being on the tour with Mark for all of ten minutes, we saw our first ghost of the evening. While he was doing his routine in bunkhouse one, his two ghostly accomplices stood outside of the bunkhouse, waiting for him to finish. His replacements were two shadowy figures that stood right behind him as he mentioned the word "spirits." One of the spirits was tall with a pushed-up hat; the other one was similar in height to Mark.

The Tunnel

The tunnel at Fort George is haunted. According to the fort guides, the little girl ghost who follows the ghost tour around will not go into the tunnel. During the day, the tunnel is passable, but at night it's a dark hellhole for those who are susceptible.

Cathy had gone through the tunnel earlier during the daytime. However, as she tried to cross the tunnel's threshold with other members of the ghost tour during the evening, she was hit by a wall of pain. She swung around as if someone had punched her in the face. Then she darted away from the tunnel entrance and kept her distance until the pain finally subsided.

One of the staff had remained outside of the tunnel. He noticed that there was a problem with Cathy. I told him that we were okay and that I would look after it. That was enough to settle his curiosity.

By now, the two boys were already at the front of the group with the tour guide. Even though our tour guide was a re-enactor at the fort, he seemed both serious and nervous that evening. Both Adam and Jacob were standing right beside him at the far end of the tunnel while he told the story of the tunnel. There were stories about ghostly troops running through the tunnel and other oddities. However, the tunnel wasn't the problem this time. It was the stairs. Adam and the guide looked up at the same time and noticed the phantom. Adam swore to me that the guide saw the phantom and tried to move from the tunnel as quickly as possible without causing absolute pandemonium. According to Adam, the spectre that they both saw was just as sinister looking as the notorious "Watcher," who haunts one of the blockhouses.

The spectre was extremely evil looking, according to Adam. He was pointing a musket with a bayonet directly at them from his position on the staircase. Adam could also make out the length of the bayonet as an American issue. He claimed that it was shorter than the British bayonet. I'm sure that this spirit made his point, as far as Adam was concerned.

Fort George   Octagonal Blockhouse

August 2005

The octagonal blockhouse, located at the most southern point of Fort George, is possibly the most haunted place in the fort. This blockhouse has three levels. It starts in the tunnel with the spiral staircase. The staircase takes you to both ground and top levels. The ground floor has a gate which allows you to return to the fort above the tunnel. This gate is usually not left open, so visitors can *enjoy* their visit to the tunnel instead. We noticed one odd thing there, just before the incident took place. It seemed strange that the gate was not open before we entered the tunnel; but after we had gone through the tunnel, the gate was left wide open for no apparent reason. Even though the open gate seemed irregular, we proceeded to climb the stairs up to the top floor which has a look-out.

The look-out was where both Cathy and Adam experienced a psychic event. During past visits, Cathy claimed that she had been drawn to a particular loophole with a view of Fort Niagara even though it made her feel queasy whenever she used it; or it gave her a strong sense of unease, if she was within close proximity to it. She claimed that both sensations were caused by an entity that stood behind her, whenever she was looking out.

This time, both Cathy and Adam were looking out of the same loophole towards Fort Niagara. They could plainly see two American ships and a major battle going on. When they looked through another loophole, they could see a peaceful landscape. After they had witnessed the vision, Cathy began to feel very poorly and I was forced to assist her from the look-out. I shouted to the boys to come down from the look-out, as we approached the ground floor. Obviously, Adam couldn't tear himself away from looking at the battle. As I shouted, Adam said the cannons went off, along with a barrage of muskets. At the same time, the outside gate to the fort slammed shut. No living person had been near it.

Could we have just witnessed a ghostly re-enactment of 1812; or were the spirits of American and British soldiers facing off against each other once again? More than likely, the armies, the ships and the battle sounds were ghostly imprints of a bygone era. The slamming of the unattended fort's gate was another matter altogether which I'll leave to your imagination.

Fort Mississauga and Fort Niagara

January 2005

We travelled to Niagara-on-the-Lake today. It was less than an hour to dusk and the weather was clear. Best of all; there was no snow on the ground. We parked alongside the golf course and walked towards Fort Mississauga which is at the mouth of the Niagara River on Lake Ontario. While approaching the old derelict fort, we could clearly hear the muskets firing from across the river at Fort Niagara, in the United States.

Fort Mississauga is a home to pigeons. They coo from their metal perches that bar the window frames and fly off, if you get too close to them. But the innocence of the pigeons in a rather large birdcage is just another decoy for the ghost hunter. It's not the pigeons or the building that the tactful hunter needs to be aware of; it's the grounds of Fort Mississauga that make this place one of the most haunted.

On a lonely winter's day, at the edge of the lake, with the sun going down; you can feel it. Even if you're not sensitive, you know that something ominous exists here. Whatever it is; it surrounds the vacant building and penetrates the frozen ground.

Jacob and I decided to explore the haunted grounds of the fort, upon arrival. We went through the lakeside tunnel, leading out to Lake Ontario. Young Jacob said something about the first settlers in Canada living on these shores. Jacob's comments made me think about how attached the first settlers were to the land.

After about five minutes, I turned around to see Cathy standing there in agony. She asked me to hold onto her because she was feeling dizzy and sick to her stomach. The dizziness and nausea got worse and she couldn't move. I had to escort her back through the lakeside tunnel, by the arm. She said that this area was particularly bad and she wanted to go to the other side of the fort. The pigeons took off in a loud flap, as we passed below one of the fort's open windows. Cathy felt much better on the other side, for a little while. She showed us her purse and asked us to feel the bottom of it. She said it was vibrating until she realized it was her hands that were tingling and vibrating.

The tingling sensation might have come from a positive source. But when violence has taken place upon the land, associated negative energies often persist to some extent. In many cases, negativity predominates.

Within a few minutes, Cathy had excruciating pain in her legs. The source of her pain had spread upwards from the ground. First, her feet and her ankles, then her legs. When I asked her what was wrong, she told me to leave her alone. Now, it really was time to leave.

Jacob noticed the other tunnel near the front entrance. He said he wouldn't go into it because it didn't seem right. As we passed in front of it, Cathy was practically in tears. Great waves of sorrow and psychic grief almost overcame her. We rushed out the front entrance and the psychic phenomena subsided. Cathy had no further problems outside of the fort.

The moat around the front of the fort was filled with mossy pools of water, long dried-out yellow stalks of old plants and tall reeds. The earth mounds were well-manicured and easy to walk upon.

Cathy and I stood at the front entrance of the fort as Adam and Jacob walked up to the top of the earth mounds to investigate the fort's defensive structure.

Adam was eleven years old and Jacob was only eight; yet, they were pacing back and forth like a couple of old soldiers. That's when something uncanny took place.

Adam claimed that the other forts were all built correctly, except for Fort Mississauga. He appeared very distinguished like Napoleon with his hands behind his back as he continued on. He maintained that the government had agreed to the original fort plan which included how the structures were to be built. Finally, he blamed the engineers for not following government specifications.

Cathy seemed amazed that Adam would know so much about how the fort was to be built. Perhaps something did happen in the past that needed to be righted; but there was not much to be done about it now.

Do you think it's possible for a senior British officer from the War of 1812 to come back as a boy to inspect his old command and to see the injustices that were committed by those who failed to hold the torch? Do you believe that he could be joined by a "bold and enterprising" junior officer who was once a guerrilla leader in the same conflict?

There was too much intrigue here for a single trip. We all agreed to investigate Fort Mississauga again in the spring.

Fort Mississauga and Fort Niagara

April 2006

The day was bright and clear. We were a little naive to think that the weather was the reason we could see Fort Niagara as a vivid close-up from Fort Mississauga. It wasn't until later that we realized that you can't normally see the soldiers on the other side of the river from Fort Mississauga with the naked eye.

A spectacular battle took place across the river at Fort Niagara that evening. Yet, there were no events scheduled after 6:30 p.m. on that day at the fort. Moreover, nothing remotely related to the French/Indians Wars had been planned for the afternoon. Even a Hollywood movie studio would not have been able to reproduce the nightmarish scene of savagery which we witnessed.

The French were defending the fort from British attackers, in a bloody and brutal show of force. Many of the British soldiers looked like battle weary highlanders. They were dressed in rags and they were backed by British Grenadiers. This is a sample of the mayhem that we saw.

A French officer with a large tricorn, sliced up a British soldier and kicked him off the fort's fortification. The officer himself became an easy target. He was shot by another British soldier and fell from his lofty position. Then a group of British soldiers stabbed a French soldier in unison with their bayonets. Several more soldiers were shot and fell from seemingly dangerous places. Throughout this hellish display of realism, muskets could be plainly heard from a particular vantage point at Fort Mississauga. Adam stated bluntly that he could barely stand to watch the hideous violence and bloodshed caused by the bayonets and the swords.

We were convinced that we had witnessed a psychic imprint of a major battle, fought almost two hundred and fifty years ago. Much of the fortification at Fort Niagara such as the earthworks and stone buildings are similar to what they were, when a major battle took place there during the 19 day siege from July 6th until July 26th in 1759. Approximately, 2500 British soldiers attacked 486 French soldiers. Could our vision be an imprint of the Battle for Fort Niagara?

During the battle a few people came into Fort Mississauga. They didn't notice any activities taking place across the river from their particular vantage-points. In one case, someone with a dog approached the earthwork. The dog started to go up the earthwork and looked up at something; then immediately changed directions. The owner said something about leaving and that the dog really didn't want to go up there anyway. Adam told me later that the dog saw something which prevented him from going to the top of the earthwork.

Stoney Creek

June 2006

After the Americans attacked Fort George, they got as far as Stoney Creek. There is a monument overlooking the battlefield there which is similar to Brock's monument. The energy fields at Stoney Creek are mixed and the bad pockets aren't as overwhelming as Queenston Heights.

On the twenty-fifth anniversary of the re-enactment of the Battle of Stoney Creek, the re-enactors and perhaps the spirits of the dead had created a high energy level on the battlefield and positive feelings all around, in spite of a wet and dreary day.

The historical Gage House was also full of positive energy. There was a real psychic sense that Sara Calder, the lady in the picture upstairs, was still around and looking after things. The basement also looked good. However, there was one problem area within the house. The kitchen re-enactors were putting on a great show of cooking biscuits; however, no one stayed very long to observe. Sadly, the kitchen had a negative psychic feeling attached to it. Fortunately, it wasn't strong enough to disrupt our enjoyment of the event.

Queenston Heights

July 25, 2006

We were prepared to leave for the Niagara area once again; but our digital camera was missing. The whole family looked for it, to no avail. Normally, it was at the bottom of the staircase on the main floor which is the most obvious and easiest place to find anything in our home. I stared at that place a few times like I was expecting it to materialize. Then Adam put some sweets down on the table and turned his back. He went to pick up the sweets again and the camera was right there beside the sweets.

Everyone got into the car. Before we left, I went back into the house and thanked the spirits for their help. They must have known that I was going to need the camera for something important.

Some people consider Queenston Heights to be the most haunted battleground in Canada. Upon our arrival, we noted that Brock's monument was fenced off for restoration purposes. We also noticed a Native American wreath on a tripod beside the fenced-off area. On closer examination, we noted that the tripod display of messages and artifacts were placed there by the ancestors of Chief Tecumseh. Native Americans have always understood that Chief Tecumseh and Brock are forever linked together in spirit.

With fewer people visiting on that day, the permeating psychic phenomena around the monument had become more pronounced and over-powering. Cathy and Adam both felt waves of nausea as they got closer to it. I rubbed Cathy's back and dangled a jet pendant around her for a minute to ease the effects of the phenomena.

We walked away for half an hour and came back. Cathy was fine until we came within range of the monument. Again, Cathy and Adam both felt sick within a few hundred feet of the monument and felt okay afterwards.

Lundy's Lane

July 25, 2006

Just after the Battle of Chippewa, another major battle took place. Many consider the Battle of Lundy's Lane to be the bloodiest to ever take place on Canadian soil. The Battle of Lundy's Lane occurred between the hours of 6:00 p.m. and 9:00 p.m. on July 25, 1814. Within this brief span of time, the British lost about 880 officers and men. The Americans lost about the same.

Today, the battlefield is a cemetery that overlooks Lundy's Lane. Although the cemetery is well posted, the traffic speeds by without a care. Once you enter the cemetery, it's easy to spot signs of vandalism. The tops of some tombs have been removed and metal plaques have been desecrated and removed in some cases. The tree carvings also seem out of place. All of this would indicate a lack of respect for the dead. Moreover, today was the anniversary of the battle; yet there was not another solitary living soul within the cemetery for the duration of our visit which lasted about forty minutes.

There's a very large tree near Lundy's Lane within the cemetery. The trunk of the tree is at least six foot wide; so the tree might have existed at the time of the battle. The tree has a fence around it, but has no plaque for identification purposes. Underneath this mighty tree, there is a hundred year anniversary monument. It was placed there in 1914, before the First World War started.

We moved towards the cenotaph and noted the names of the British soldiers who fell in the Battle of Lundy's Lane. After looking at the names, Cathy felt that there were still some scattered bones under the old tree and throughout the cemetery; nevertheless, the King's colours proudly flew over the cenotaph and everything there seemed in order.

We moved away from the cenotaph towards some other gravestones which Cathy seemed to be attracted to. We noticed that twenty American soldiers and an identified American officer had recently been found and had been put to rest within the cemetery.

As we looked at the stones, Cathy said to me, "Can't you feel it?"

I knew what she meant and I said that I didn't feel the same way, as she walked slowly away.

Adam knew the story of the unknown American soldiers. They had found the bones of the soldiers quite recently. In fact, the President of the United States had been contacted. I was interested in what Adam had to say and I didn't notice that Cathy had walked over to the bench to sit down. She seemed to be weighed down with something rather heavy. Adam went over to her and sat beside her. I sat on the other side of the bench.

I was looking a bit towards Cathy, when a branch about three feet long appeared in front of us and hit her on the head. The branch did not fall from anywhere. Instead, we all saw the branch materialize out of nowhere like some phantom bird with flapping wings. I examined the branch and noted that it looked very much like it had been sliced off with a sharp blade. I decided to test my theory. The branch was about half an inch thick. When I bent the branch, the wood shattered. Therefore, it was highly unlikely that the branch broke off naturally, or could have flown across the cemetery in search of a target. Rather, the branch was teleported by a spirit with malice aforethought, with the intention of hitting Cathy on the head.

We walked away from the bench towards the other side of the cemetery and discovered more American graves. It was a very hot day. If you took the humidity into consideration, it felt like it was forty degrees Celsius; yet, Cathy, Adam and Jacob all felt like they were in ice water. Cathy was shaking uncontrollably and had to be held up. She was on the verge of collapse just before we got her out of the cemetery. Instead of running out of the cemetery, she maintained her decorum like the proud lady that she was and with a little help from Adam and myself we assisted her to a bench at the far end of the cemetery, away from the graves. She described the experience as the worst she had encountered at any fort or any battlefield.

Later that day, I asked her about the difference between the two sites that we had visited that day. Cathy just said that Queenston Heights felt "strange and weird," but there was something else in Lundy's Lane cemetery besides bones and graves.

As we returned home with our memories of the day, Cathy had the same involuntary, sad sensation which she gets when she leaves the Niagara area. Even after she arrives home, she still feels the loss. She doesn't know what causes it and she has no control over it.

Haunted Fort Niagara

Orbs in Haunted Places

If you ever intend to visit a haunted historical site, you may be interested in how the soul gets around in the earthly dimension after its physical, material life has ended.

There is evidence to suggest that human spirits use orbs to transport themselves from place to place and that real orbs can be sensed and heard. The Egyptians described true orbs as "sun boats." They were referred to in the Old Testament as "Merkabah." The Merkabah has also been described in the Kaballah and other Jewish schools of mysticism. Moreover, the prophet Ezekial associated the Merkabab with the heavenly realms.

George Michael in his e-book Colors of the Soul claims that real orbs make a super-high tone that is heard chiefly in the head, beyond normal hearing. Many individuals who have encountered true orbs have experienced the orb speaking telepathically to them.

According to Michael, orbs can assume many appearances, including various sizes of spherical bodies and circular light patterns. They also range in degrees of illumination from bright and glowing to faded and barely visible. Michael's research into orbs also suggests that the human spirit-type orbs are usually seen at about eye level, to about ceiling height and are often filmed in graveyards and haunted locations. There are even accounts of orbs which have more detailed and complex appearances which may at times contain figures or faces. These particular orbs are usually associated with higher spiritual beings; since they are only seen on rare occasions.

Professional photographer Gregory Avery has captured thousands of orb images on film. He noted that orbs are seldom viewed by either photographers or subjects until they appear on the developed film. They same can be said about digital prints and images. There is plenty of evidence to suggest that orbs are often present at festive occasions such as anniversaries and solemn occasions such as funerals and memorial services. They may also be found at cemeteries, haunted houses and sacred places.

Psychic Awareness

Truth telling dreams are as old as the Bible itself. There is plenty of evidence from Old Testament times and onwards that dreams were regarded as the one means of communication between the Divinity and the human race.

More recently, people with so called "psychic perception" speak of such natural things as "second sight" or "sixth sense." Many so-called "fortune tellers," with greater or less success, claim that they can tell the present or the future to some extent. Fortune tellers or psychics use such aids as crystals, tarot cards and tea leaves in the telling of various futures.

Given that there are different levels of awareness among psychics themselves, couldn't one presuppose that we are all, to some extent psychic? This way of knowing is based on one's intuition, since it comes from within. Like many other activities in life, psychic awareness can be developed through trial and error. To begin training, you must separate your own beliefs and others' opinions, from your "inner voice." This is done by being calm and reflective; thereby allowing your intuition to take over.

Developing your psychic abilities may provide a means to prove to yourself that there are negative or positive elements within particular environments. Nevertheless, a warning to the curious is necessary. Being intuitive and overly sensitive to psychic phenomena, also invites unexpected psychic feedback.

Accordingly, before one enters into any haunted site, one should be aware of the violence associated with it.

A Brief History of Fort Niagara

La Salle made it here in 1678 and built the first structure; but the Seneca didn't think much of its defenses and burnt it down in 1689. A new two-story building was built on the same site in 1726. This permanent structure has the distinction of being the oldest building in North American's Great Lakes area. The building, later known as the "French Castle," was built to resemble a trading post, so that the Iroquois were not offended. They thought of the trading post as a "house of peace;" but they were never invited inside. They would not have been amused, if they had found out that the French fortifications could easily have withstood a primitive attack.

The fort was expanded to its present size in 1755, due to increased tensions between French and British colonial interests. The French lost control of the fort, after a 19 day siege in 1759. The British commanded Fort Niagara until 1796, before turning it over to the Americans. However, the British Redcoats took it back on a bitterly, cold December evening in 1813 in retaliation, for the burning of Newark and the destruction of York. After the War of 1812, Fort Niagara was ceded to the United States for the 2nd time and there were no more armed conflicts.

The First Visit to Fort Niagara

The fates had decided that it was time to make our first pilgrimage to the haunted citadel, on a clear and cold late autumn day. We passed through two gates to enter the fort; one gate being British and the other gate being French. The fort was expansive with the impressive castle blending in. Each section of the fort vied for our attention and we enjoyed the fort's formidable defensive positions from each vantage point. The most impressive one was the view of the mouth of the Niagara River with the pale, grey waters of Lake Ontario in the background.

Hundreds of school children had been at the fort earlier, for a special day event. After the children left, we were lucky enough to have some excellent re-enactors to talk with in the afternoon. All of the re-enactors were staying at the fort overnight because there were more activities scheduled for the next day. Therefore, the re-enactors were keen on sustaining an 18th century North American colonial fort atmosphere throughout our visit.

We were rewarded in many ways. The troops did their drills in French "manual style." They also did several cannon firings just for us and a couple of other people. In fact, we had their undivided attention for the entire afternoon.

Sometimes re-enactors engage in "military activities" for their own entertainment, in the same way that regular soldiers try to make their training as realistic as possible. One of our soldier hosts recalled that last year, he had to deal with a surprise attack. Just as he was turning in for the evening, his fellow re-enactors from the other side of the fort became turncoats and decided to attack his section.

Besides the unexpected, the normal rigors of a soldier's life at Fort Niagara would include trying to stay warm. Because of Fort Niagara's location, the waves of Lake Ontario smash the shore line, so hard at times, that the freezing spray comes up over the walls and onto the parade ground. After some woeful tales of frozen guards and inclement weather, I could feel winter's icy cold fingers reaching out for me also; so I tried on a heavy grey French winter coat which temporarily took the chill out of my bones. I was told that the coat could also withstand a lot of moisture. I heartily agreed. Reluctantly, I gave the heavy French overcoat back to the re-enactor and it wasn't long before everything started to go numb again.

In spite of the cold weather, we didn't notice the time passing by. Daylight savings was in effect and it would be dark within the hour. But before we left, we were determined to visit the French Castle.

The French Castle

There are dozens of ghost tour operators who would like to be the official source of supernatural lore at the fort. From our perspective, formalized ghost tours should be regarded as entertainment, rather than an opportunity to record paranormal phenomena.

With regard to whether or not there are ghost at Fort Niagara, the people in the know will tell you that the place is haunted, without any prompting at all. There are reliable volunteer soldiers who have seen phantoms here and they believe in them. It gives you the shudders on a chilly fall day, just hearing from someone you don't expect to believe in such things, to say to you that there are phantoms at Fort Niagara.

There was one phantom which the re-enactors had followed down the stairs one day, after everything was locked up from the outside after hours. The phantom just disappeared. Another incident occurred at night in the same building; but this time, the phantom soldier escaped by walking through the wall.

The re-enactors don't mind sleeping in some parts of the fort; but it is still a daunting task to spend the night in the old castle. Nevertheless, there was someone who didn't know any better, wanted to try it on their own. They were told that everything would be locked up and there was no way to get out until the morning. Still, this strong-minded individual was determined to spend the night in the French Castle. This may sound a lot like the film "Web of the Spider" in which someone wagered a bet that they could spend the night in a haunted house. But in this case, the individual's bravado turned to apprehension, after he heard some footsteps and other sinister noises in the building, within thirty minutes of his arrival. The result was that he completely lost his nerve. Fortunately, he had a cell phone and the fort manager's hotline number. His desperate call for help was not totally unexpected and thanks to an understanding manager, he was able to elude the phantoms.

Before we knew it, it was closing time. Cathy felt a very strong urge to investigate the upper levels of the castle, but we had to leave. I reassured her that we would be back again very soon.

In summary, we identified psychic phenomena in three main areas. The first was the fort area on the Niagara River which includes the powder magazine and the cannons. In general, almost everything on the river side of the fort produced negative psychic feelings.

The second area was the kitchen which was right next to the French Castle. Cathy's camera battery showed that it was completely drained while she was inside the kitchen. After leaving the building, the camera showed that it was fully charged which was not surprising given that she had just put a new battery in the camera.

We faced a similar situation while visiting a church near Cambridge, England. This particular English church was a place where many people had fled to, in order to escape the Black Plague. But unfortunately, the plague spread within the church. Hence, the church became more of a tomb than a sanctuary.

While going up the church tower's spiral staircase, I tried to take a picture several times; but my camera wouldn't function. It was probably the most bizarre thing which had happened to me up until that point in my life. I didn't believe in ghosts at the time; yet, there was no logical explanation for what happened. The fear that was created in my mind from a lack of understanding was the main reason I left the tower. Shortly thereafter, I arrived in the churchyard, where upon my camera started to work again. We weren't at the French Castle very long before we realized that it belonged to the ghosts. Our newfound re-enactor friend with a rather awe-inspiring hat had just told us some true ghost stories; but admitted that the story of the French soldier who was beheaded following swordplay over a beautiful Native American maiden was really a false account. The story goes that his chopped-up body was rumored to have been thrown down the well, just inside the French Castle. His head was thrown into Lake Ontario.

Just remember that doesn't mean there isn't a headless ghost in the fort. If a headless ghost should actually appear, I doubt whether there will be any need for embellishment in retelling the incident.

Then our friend noticed that his wig was getting twisted around for some bizarre reason; so he took his great hat off to adjust it. That's when Cathy noticed a yellow orb about the size of a baseball just behind the re-enactor's head. Because of my light clothing, I was more concerned about controlling my shaking body from the biting air to notice anything. Meanwhile, Cathy had adjusted her glasses to make sure that it wasn't sunlight. But after the re-enactor adjusted his wig, the orb suddenly disappeared. Both Adam and Jacob also saw the yellow orb floating about.

The next day, I researched the internet for any ghostly reports at Fort Niagara. I read about a similar account at the French Castle. The incident was witnessed at a later hour by a fairly high-level official at the fort and was published on October 20, 2002 by the St. Petersburg Times.

Here is a quote of what took place in the French Castle a few years before:

> He entered the dark hallway, he said and waited. At first there was nothing."Then, there it was … it seemed to move across the hallway, just about head-level. It was yellowish, and about the size of a softball."

Needless to say, the official fled in fear and admitted that the incident left him shaken. The main difference in our sighting was that it took place in broad daylight as the sun was setting. It was about 4:15 p.m. and we were situated just inside the French Castle's main door, by the well. It was very gloomy in there, but there was still plenty of daylight. As I recall, the re-enactor had given us a demonstration of how the trap door on the main gate could be used to provide security, if you wanted to keep your bayonet on someone you didn't trust. In other words, someone could be made to crawl through the lower part of the door; thereby exposing their back to one's bayonet.

His wig appeared to be secure and in place during the demonstration. Perhaps the spirits played a prank on him after the demonstration.

One thing we do know for sure is that our re-enactor friend was blissfully unaware of the floating orb. As a result, he continued on with his stories unabated until closing time.

We left Fort Niagara with regret. As we drove back across the border and headed north, Cathy felt the most overwhelming sense of loss. Her feelings of belonging to an area had never been this strong before. Later on, she said she had a strong connection with the original Europeans who came here. Only time will tell.

The Second Visit to Fort Niagara

We returned to Fort Niagara a few weeks later. It was less windy; but overcast. The desolate, cool sky and grey lapping waves greeted us like long lost friends. This time there was only a skeleton staff to entertain us. The lone re-enactor at the fort started out doing his presentation inside the provisions storehouse which is right next door to a heated office. After everyone had warmed their bones sufficiently, it was time to move outside. In spite of the damp chill, we were treated to an excellent musket demonstration and some parade ground maneuvers.

Our first visit to the fort was for pleasure. This time we meant business. Although we were very lucky to have several re-enactors available on our first visit, it was imperative that we were not disturbed by other visitors while touring the fort for psychic evidence. Nor did we want to attract attention to ourselves, which was more likely to happen.

This was our first visit to the provisions storehouse which was built by the British. Adam was attracted to the metal display stand in a corner. There were many interesting plates of soldiers on exhibit. Adam commented on some of the uniform details, in addition to some of the excellent drawings.

There was a large table in the centre of the room which showed the topographical make-up of the area. Cathy kept looking at the table area while she tried to concentrate on Adam's comments. She was distracted because of a shadowy figure which she could see out of the corner of her eye. When she looked directly at the shadow, it would disappear.

The powder magazine was open for viewing, even though it was being renovated. The main feature of the building was the strong semi-circular arch which was engineered to withstand a heavy bombardment, and the main attraction appeared to be a large bronze bust of Samuel de Champlain. We were interested in examining the bust; but the psychic atmosphere of the building was so oppressive that we had to leave in a hurry.

The bake house which the British built from the remains of the French bakery had a similar psychic feeling to it. It was unwelcoming and somewhat oppressive. Nevertheless, we were able to take a couple of pictures this time.

Our Return to the French Castle

The lower level of the French Castle was comprised of various storerooms, a bakery and the trading post. Because we were attracted to the exhibition of goods at the trading post, it seemed like the right place to start. A large birch bark canoe hung overhead, and a few token pelts of animal furs were seen. Furs were so plentiful back in those days that there would have been a large stockpile of them. Instead, native trading goods such as flashy trinkets and tomahawks were on display.

As we left the trading post, we passed by the well in the vestibule. Adam noticed the Sun King's picture hanging on the back wall, behind the well. He seemed to have a problem with it; but he didn't say anything about it at the time.

On our first visit, Cathy was drawn to the second floor; but we had to leave the fort prematurely because the sun was setting and it was closing time. This time we were able to take a few pictures of the children in the bakery and in some of the other ground level rooms.

After a short tour of the bottom floor, we climbed the thick wooden steps up to the second story vestibule. The barracks and the chapel came into view. The chapel; plus the top level were the two places which Cathy was mainly attracted to. There was also a sacristy behind the chapel; but it was not open to the public.

The Jesuit chapel was very attractive: with an altar, a large cross and a Christ figure. Nevertheless, there was a strong negative presence within the room. We were captivated by the sacred symbols; yet, we were repelled by the spiritual forces around us. Reluctantly, Cathy was forced to leave the chapel due to the psychic negativity. Her forced withdrawal was also a personal disappointment given that she had been looking forward to this visit.

We walked over the other side of the second story floor, towards the barracks. Everything there seemed to be in order; so we proceeded to the north side which had some great views of Lake Ontario. In fact, the officers had their apartments on the lake side. That's when Adam noticed some of the art-work. There were a few paintings of his favourite historical figures like Lieutenant Governor Simcoe and Colonel Butler of Butler's Rangers; but for the most part, he disliked the images which he saw. He claimed that the paintings on the wall had a certain unreality about them. According to Adam, most of the depictions of historical figures at Fort Niagara seemed to look back and follow him around.

At some point, Adam started to make comments about Louis XIV, also known as the Sun King of France. Adam knew French history and he did not like Louis XIV. The king was dead and his portrait was out of sight on the ground floor; so technically he had nothing to worry about. But we were in and around the officers' apartments, in a French castle, held by the French, at the time of Louis XIV. Given that there just might be ghosts around, it would be a sure bet that some of them might be French. After our cool reception in the chapel, I was surprised that Adam would lay into the Sun King without consideration for the dead. Now, I was hoping that he had a plan, just in case. Adam continued to comment about the paintings, even as we admired the centuries old furniture and the elaborate designs of the French Castle.

After we had visited all of the apartments and the officers' kitchen, there was still one more place to investigate. Cathy re-entered the second level vestibule. She walked over to the stairs and looked upwards towards the third level. Then she moved forward and climbed the stairs in a determined manner.

We fell into step behind her like lemmings walking towards a sea cliff. There was no turning back now. Whatever had been waiting for her to return to the fort was up on the third level.

The third level was distinctly cooler. It was basically one large room; so you could easily see the entire third level. There was a ladder leading up to the roof and some well-hidden loopholes which allowed fresh air inside. There wasn't much to see in the room itself, but everyone was very much aware that the third level environment was different from the rest of the castle.

Cathy tried to take a few pictures. The digital camera had worked everywhere so far, except when she tried to take a picture of the ladder. She tried five times without success. I focused on the ladder and imposed my will upon it. I told her that the camera would work. She took the picture. We reviewed our results on the camera's viewer. There were several visible orbs by the ladder.

By then, the psychic atmosphere of the third floor had begun to deteriorate significantly. Both the boys and Cathy were now aware of the oppressive nature of the third level. Adam got out his penny whistle which he had brought to the fort with him. He began to play the "Hanover Hornpipe." Things began to ease a bit. Not content with the first tune, Adam launched into a battle call, the "British Grenadiers." This tune was often associated with comfort and courage and has rallied the British troops for centuries. After the second tune, the malevolence completely disappeared. Adam had just finished playing the final note when he stopped abruptly.

Someone who worked at the fort had rushed up the stairs and had appeared at the top level with a ghastly pale look of fright about him. The expression on his face was of utter relief and his body seemed to relax after a half minute or so of tension. He said, "I thought you were," but he never finished the statement.

We knew perfectly well that he meant "ghosts." After the shock of seeing real people there, he admitted that he had heard the tune of the British Grenadiers from this place before. Obviously, there had been no one on the third level when he arrived the last time.

Then he apologized and seemed to be happy to leave the third floor. I asked Adam why he selected the "Hanover Hornpipe" and the "British Grenadiers;" since he knew how to play dozens of songs. He claimed that the sounds of each melody came into his head before he played them. As such, he strongly felt that the inspiration came from beyond.

Because of our success on the third floor, I felt that we should have another go at the chapel. I knew that Cathy would be disappointed if we didn't try again. Adam played another tune upon entering the chapel. This one was called "Worship the King." This time Adam said that he had an even stronger feeling that he should play a particular melody. He claimed it was almost like a command.

It seemed like a miracle, but the chapel changed completely from a place of malevolence to a place of joy and pleasantries. Everyone enjoyed their visit and we all walked away in good faith.

If I didn't know better, I would hypothesize that the French control the second floor and the British invaders still occupy the top floor. The spirits of British soldiers may still be protecting Fort George from an attack. Perhaps they haven't forgotten the Americans soldiers at Fort Niagara who sought to destroy Fort George during the War of 1812.

The Final Haunting

Before our exit out of the fort, we decided to go under the earthwork walls to investigate the scarp walls and casemate gallery. It was quite dingy in this area, even with the sunlight streaming through the cannon loopholes. Adam charged ahead. Unfortunately for him, the corridor narrowed and he banged his head on something. I didn't get much beyond the end of the stairs before I had to shout out to Adam to come back. Cathy had not moved a step beyond the stairs leading down. She was in a terrible state and everyone had a headache, except me of course. Adam thought that his headache was from banging his head; but it soon dawned on him that the real problem was the location. We all got out of there as quickly as possible. I also had to help Cathy up the stairs. She said she couldn't breathe. She said later that it was like someone was sitting on her chest.

After I made sure that everyone was okay, I asked Cathy for her camera and I ran down the stairs and took the perfect ghost picture. I returned promptly with the evidence. There were many orbs showing on the camera viewer.

The scarp walls and casemate gallery were built during the American Civil War. Still, it's possible that there were casualties near these walls, when the British dug their tunnels towards the fort in 1759. Or perhaps, with all of the French and British spirits occupying the French Castle, it's also possible that some of the American casualties from the War of 1812 were still attached to the cannons. Anyone who has ever considered moving cannons from Fort Niagara to somewhere else should be advised.

Further Evidence

After reviewing the digital pictures at home, there were many more orbs than expected. For example, I only took one photo and there were at least six orbs clearly showing within the casemate gallery area.

Even though the scarp walls and casemate gallery area appeared to be the most malevolent place in the fort, the French Castle appeared to be the most haunted building. There was one huge orb about one foot in diameter right beside me in the officers' apartments. Several other rooms such as the officers' mess and the second-floor powder magazine also had orbs about. The chapel had several orbs, including one by the large cross.

The third-floor area provided us with more evidence of psychic phenomena. Several digital pictures taken there revealed numerous orbs. One of our photos needed to be enlarged. The photo showed me standing in the shadows, just to the right of a thick wooden support with the wall behind me. I was shocked to see several human sized faces protruding from the support. Besides this totem pole of ghostly faces, there was at least one face projecting from the wall, behind my right shoulder.

I didn't publish the picture until many years later (Shadow Moon, 2021 p.160). The face behind my shoulder had a very large evil smile. The face also had a jester hat on. That image disappeared from the digital print which I had. After looking at the image originally, I didn't want to publish it. Cathy also told me not to publish it. The jester reminded me of the devil himself, and I doubt if the soldiers would have wanted their picture taken with him.

After counting a few dozen orbs and ghostly faces throughout the fort, a concerned Adam finally admitted to his folly in challenging the king of France. Moreover, based on our evidence we sincerely hope that any individual who decides to spend the night alone in the French Castle will appreciate our findings.

The Haunted Forts and Battlefields of 1812

(July 2007 – July 2009)

Fort Mississauga

July 7th, 2007

The most violent conflicts during the War of 1812 occurred in the Niagara area. The first two places we visited during the summer of 2007 were both destroyed by the American forces on May 27, 1813.

Point Mississauga or Fort Mississauga as it is called today was strategically located at the mouth of the Niagara River just across the water from the American fort. The battery here was destroyed after firing just one shot, on the morning of May 27, 1813. Another battery at Two Mile Creek, just a bit further along the lake shore from Point Mississauga was also abandoned about the same time.

The America forces landed at Two Mile Creek and a major engagement took place with the odds being four American soldiers to one British soldier. Within a distance of ten yards, at point blank range, the soldiers from both sides fired away. Within fifteen minutes, there were over one hundred dead bodies piled up on top of one and another. Hundreds more would be killed within hours.

The retreating British blew up the main magazine at Fort George and abandoned the fort later on that day, after an intense bombardment by the Americans.

* * *

It was warm and slightly overcast day, with a pleasant breeze. Across the Niagara River, there was a French Indian Wars re-enactment at Fort Niagara. Fort Mississauga, on the other hand, was deserted for the hour that we were at the fort, except for two people other than ourselves, who went to the lake shore for a viewing; then quickly left. Perhaps they weren't that keen on staying. After today's dramatic events, I'm not sure that I will ever want to return to the haunted grounds of Fort Mississauga either.

We entered the fort and there was the usual grim psychic feelings attached to it. I gave Cathy my personal jet pendant to help protect her. We went through a tunnel and took the steps down to the lake side.

There was Adam, Jacob, Cathy and myself. Cathy felt a presence nearby, as she turned around and snapped a shot at the pathway which we had just descended. She was in total disbelief as she noted the ghost staring back at her through the viewfinder. Adam said that he looked like George Washington, or of that time. Once everyone settled down, I asked her to take another picture. This time she got another spirit who was frowning. We took a third picture and the spirit was smiling at us. This spirit was also dressed in the attire of the French Indian Wars.

From that point onwards, Cathy was harassed by the spirits. She was even slapped as she tried to take another picture. Later on, Adam commented that it was likely a French officer from Fort Niagara. Adam had made uncomplimentary remarks about the Sun King at the fort the year before. Perhaps the French Indian war re-enactment across the water had rejuvenated the officer enough to seek redress. When we walked into his trap, he was delighted to entertain us in our foolish adventure. Or so it would seem.

Afterwards, we moved away from the lake and sat down near the main building. Everything was peaceful for a while, until Jacob wandered over towards one of the dark tunnels inside the mounds. He stated that he saw an evil looking face staring back out at him. Adam wanted me to go into the other tunnel and take a picture. I took a picture of the beam which wasn't two feet from my face. I knew that there would be a spirit there. Even though we didn't see the picture until we got home, it was the same spirit that scared Jacob a few minutes before. The face appeared to be a Native American from the time of the French Indian Wars.

We walked back to the car and continued on into town for a bit. I had some groceries to take back to the car while Cathy and the boys decided to visit one more shop.

While I was waiting for them back at the car, I decided to look through Adam's books. I found a copy of Osprey: "The American War – 1812-14." I started flipping through it until I got to page 18. There was a photo of a flag. It was the 13th Infantry Regiment. The flag showed an eagle and a coat of arms related to the regiment. At the time I didn't have that much information on the 13th. The book only said that the 13th regiment was part of a larger American force which had left the Plattsburg area for the Niagara frontier. When I got home I found out that the 13th regiment had been the main force which had crossed the Niagara River to Queenston Heights on October 13, 1812. It may seem somewhat ironic that the 13th regiment crossed the Niagara River on the 13th. Moreover, thirteen large boats were used to ferry the American troops across the river. Even though the 13th regiment was the first to strike at the British in the Niagara area, they had a lot of bad luck that day because their reinforcements did not arrive.

The 13th regiment was also responsible for General Brock's death. Had Brock lived, Chief Tecumseh might have had his Indian nation. It would never be the same without Brock.

In Adam's book, blood had dripped on the flag of the 13th regiment. Even though the book had been shut, the blood was not found on any other page, so it must have dried instantly. The blood was a bright crimson colour. There were a several smears on the flag. It really looked like someone didn't care about the flag. Perhaps, the anger directed at the 13th regiment had survived two centuries.

When Adam got back to the car, he was shocked. He stated that the book had been okay when he packed it.

We were parked about fifty feet from the golf course. It was a five minute walk over the golf course to the fort. However, I could smell something odd in the car. I tried to use the jet; but someone didn't like my idea. That's when Cathy's leg got smacked.

The window on the driver's side was down, and my arm was resting there. Right after Cathy got smacked; I was stabbed in the arm. My arm felt like it had be stung by a very poisonous bee. I checked for a bee sting, but my arm was perfectly fine. There was no mark or redness showing. Plus, there was no lingering pain which happens with a proper bee sting. It may sound daft to say, but the sting really felt more like the sharp end of a bayonet.

On the way home there was an atrociously bad air smell. It happened about every twenty minutes, and it would not stop. I tried the jet each time; but I couldn't control it.

Finally, we arrived home. Cathy was ice cold. Jacob went to the washroom, but he came out in a state of panic. Someone had touched him on the shoulder. I had to calm him down. I knew that a spirit had come back with us. I used my crystal healing rod and the power of light. Jacob said that the spirit had the same power as the healing rod and that he could counter it; but he was no match for the white light which I had requested to help me charge the healing rod.

Cathy had a terrific headache by that point in time; but she could sense where the spirit was. The spirit was right beside me. She asked me for the healing rod and then she pointed it at him. The spirit was removed.

Cathy also had a strong visual impression of the spirit before he was dispatched. She asked me for a pencil and paper and sketched an image of him. Afterwards, Jacob told me that the power of the light had sent the spirit back to the fort or to the light. He wasn't sure exactly where. He also said that we were protected from him.

Cathy said that there are always will be spirits that harbour grudges for whatever reason. In brief, grudges that were created *centuries ago* are still with us today.

Note: On a further note of harbouring grudges, I had a drawing of the 13th's regimental flag that I wanted to include in this publication. We scanned over fifty drawings without any problem whatsoever. When we got to the regimental flag of the 13th everything was the same as the other drawings, except the results of the scan were cut off so that you only had half of the flag. After more than half a dozen attempts on different occasions, I told Cathy that the spirits did not want this flag in my book. The scanning of the 13th's regimental flag took place three years after the original incident, but it didn't matter. I would argue that there was more hatred directed at this American regiment than any other during the War of 1812. The spirits made this point quite clear. Nothing has changed.

Fort George

July 16, 2007

It was another pleasant, slightly overcast day as we wandered into the first blockhouse on our route. Cathy told me that the spirit in the first blockhouse did not like the changes in the fort. Mind you, they had put a display right in front of the window where the famous Watcher liked to look out. One staffer got more than he bargained for when he challenged the Watcher to appear. The terrified staffer left town in a big hurry. He stayed just long enough to deliver one last warning: *Don't challenge the Watcher*.

After visiting the first blockhouse, we walked up to the southern end of the fort because we knew that was where the real action was. We had just gone around the end of a building where maintenance staff had been working on boats and equipment when Cathy stopped. She had a beautiful smile on her face. In fact, she looked like she had found heaven. She said that she was incredibly happy and that she didn't want to leave the fort. Jacob touched her and she lost contact with the spirit before I had a chance to question her. It was very disappointing because I had never seen her so happy before. Cathy's experience changed my whole perspective on the nature of spirits. Fort George seemed like the last place for this to happen. I was expecting pain and suffering, not bliss.

We continued on towards the tunnel. Cathy followed us. After Cathy took a few pictures, we went up the spiral staircase to the ground level and walked out onto the grass. Adam began to play *British Grenadiers* on his fife. There was a problem and I found his playing to be disturbing. He attempted to play it again.

He told me that someone was controlling his playing and he couldn't play properly. Moreover, he tried to play *Chain Cotillion* the old way with one different note, but the spirit would not allow him to play the note the way he wanted to play it. Adam stopped playing. He went to the top of the octagonal blockhouse where he could play the note the way he wanted to play it.

We drove by Fort Mississauga on the way home. Cathy said to me that she thought it looked clearer than usual. After leaving the Niagara area, we all experienced a very heavy sulfuric smell that continued for a mile or so. Every time the smell came back, it was worse than before. The second time, the smell was worse than a sewer. The third time, the smell was like the guts of hell. I tried to get rid of it with the jet. I failed.

I didn't waste any time after I arrived home. I used my two power rods to sanitize our home from the negativity. It worked. Cathy said that there was no indication of any problems in our home.

Fort York

July 20, 2007

On April 27, 1813, the American forces attacked York before the British could complete their defenses. Because of the confusion created by the attack, several British companies were sent out against the Americans in piecemeal fashion. They were cut down one at a time in quick succession. Because the best trained and experienced British soldiers had already been sent out against the Americans at the beginning of the battle, British General Shaeffe lost command of his remaining troops.

The British flag was left flying as the Americans approached the fort. The Americans, under the command of General Pike, were under the impression that the British were still inside; so they proceeded to the edge of the fort. However, the British had already left. As the British retreated, they lit a fuse within the stone magazine. A horrific blast from the stored gun powder destroyed most of the fort and killed General Pike.

Because there were several hundred casualties that day from both the fighting and the massive explosion, one would expect Fort York to be severely haunted. Nevertheless, we found the fort a bit benign compared to other battlefields. Cathy said that it is partly because the fort was closer to the waterfront during the War of 1812. The waterfront had shifted a great deal and the battlefield was now spread out over a larger area. Accordingly, one might find that there are haunted places in and around Fort York.

We started our tour with the Officers' Mess. The commanding officer of the fort had been seen by more than one person; so we felt we should pay our respects to him first of all.

A spirit in the archeology block house was interested in what we had to say about the artifacts there, so he made his presence known.

The small fur room which had recently been established in the Junior Officers' Barracks was more like the basement under the Officers' Mess from a psychic's point of view. Perhaps the fur room didn't go over very well with the junior officers.

Fort Malden

August 2, 2007

Fort Malden was called Fort Amherstburg during the War of 1812. The fort was situated at Amherstburg, along side the Detroit River. Tecumseh and Brock had their first victories against the Americans at the beginning of the War of 1812 in this area. However, in 1813, the British lost the Battle of Lake Erie and from that point on, their supply route was more or less cut off. The British decided to burn Fort Amherstburg in September of 1813 and retreat up the Thames. The Americans were in hot pursuit. The final result was the Battle of the Thames where Tecumseh was killed.

We toured the two floored museum at Fort Malden and noted several items related to Tecumseh, including his powder horn. Shortly afterwards, we continued on with our journey, to the battlefield.

The Battlefield near Moraviantown, Ontario

August 2, 2007

The battleground was marked by a small park and two stone memorials. The older stone was a bit worn. The larger memorial had a plaque, a picture of Tecumseh and some tribal markings.

The park ran along the steep banks of the Thames. There was a dirt road alongside the park which was several hundred feet long. On the other side of the dirt road, there was a grassy area with trees. For most of the length of the road, the grassy area was narrow. Bordering the grassy area was a huge corn field. Even with the maps that I brought with me; it was difficult to imagine what a battlefield in 1813 would have looked like.

* * *

The Battle of the Thames has been described in several accounts. Tecumseh chose the best defensive position he could find. Instead of a corn field you have to imagine a large swamp beyond the corn field and some thick woods bordering the swamp. In front of the large swamp, there was a small swamp near the River Thames. Back in 1813 a road ran alongside the Thames. The 41st Regiment of Foot of the Right Division and other British auxiliaries stayed close to the road while the Native Americans under Tecumseh spread out, in a semi-circular flank to the British.

The Americans were bold in their attack. They attacked all flanks and even charged through the small swamp. They outnumbered the British and their allies by a fair amount, so a wild charge was not unthinkable under the circumstances.

It's a well-known fact that Tecumseh knew that he would not survive the battle. Apparently, he was talking with some British officers when a shot came out of nowhere and he doubled up in pain like he had been shot. The shot never happened. No one fired a musket; yet everyone heard it. He told the officers that a bad spirit was present. It was also a premonition of what was to take place.

* * *

We had no problem parking right in front of the two stone memorials. But I still needed to figure out where the battlefield was located, so we walked the length of the dirt road and back again. Cathy had no feeling for the place and she knew nothing of the battlefield; but she said that there wasn't much around the memorial site. She added that we needed to move away from the memorial site and go towards the corn field.

After we crossed the dirt road, there were a few crab apple trees. I asked Cathy to take pictures of them. That's when Cathy and Adam both began to feel nauseated. Cathy also had problems taking pictures. We had two digital cameras and one of them was brand new. Cathy had just taken several pictures without any problem over by the memorial site and now she was having problems.

I suggested that we move further towards the battlefield in the direction of Tecumseh's native warriors as we understood it. There were several pine trees which bordered the large grassy area along side the corn field. Cathy was almost at the limit of what she could stand by now; plus she was having a great deal of difficulty in taking any pictures at this point. The camera would not work in one particular area at all.

It had been a windless, hot day. We had been outside much of the time and there had been very little breeze. We had also been in the park for over half an hour and there had been no indication that the weather would change. It was about 6:30 p.m. when the winds began to blow quite hard. Perhaps this witch's wind materialized because Cathy had tried to take a picture of a pine tree. I knew that the spirits would be close to the trees; but the reaction was stronger than I expected. At that point, we had to retreat from the battlefield.

Back at the memorial site, Cathy was still having problems taking pictures. We managed to take a few extra pictures, but after experiencing some negative pockets of energy on the battlefield, we thought it might be more prudent to leave before something else developed.

The air temperature that day was over 30 degrees Celsius. I had barely driven the car onto the main highway when Cathy said that she was ice cold and her skin was all goosebumps. She also said that there was a spirit with us. I took out my jet pendant and said to the spirit that Tecumseh demanded that all warriors should stay on the battlefield. Cathy said that the spirit vanished the moment I said that.

Upon reflection, we figured that the battlefield was still very haunted and that it should be a national heritage site. Growing corn on a battlefield is one thing; wishing the spirits to go away is quite another.

The Canadian government almost made the same mistake with Chippewa. Fortunately, the right decision was made and it is now a place of honour.

Fort Erie

August 13, 2007

Fort Erie was placed under siege by the British in 1814. A daring night time raid on August 14, 1814, by the British resulted in the magazine blowing up. The British were less protected. More than nine hundred British soldiers were either wounded or lost as a result of the blast. The Americans attacked the British a few days later and there were still more casualties on both sides. With the loss of an additional 565 British soldiers, British General Drummond did not have enough forces to attack the fort again. A few months later, the Americans abandoned the fort.

Many soldiers were hastily buried near Fort Erie around the time of the 1814 siege. In fact, nearby Snake Hill provided archaeologists with a significant find of American skeleton bodies. The skeletons' bodies which were found sometimes lacked arms, legs and even heads. Some of this was attributed to battlefield medicine. However, it's also conceivable that many more bodies were blown to pieces and never found because of the massive explosion which occurred in 1814. We believe that the spirits who had no proof of their dead bodies may also have had some difficulty realizing that they were dead. The same spirits were also more likely to haunt the fort.

I went straight up the Officers' Quarters to experience it; since I knew it was haunted. There were many instances of Cathy's camera not being able to take pictures. If the ghosts wouldn't let her take the picture, they would allow Adam to do the honours. A few times, a ghost got in front of Cathy's shots. They made it look like a triangular flag which covered half of the shot.

Most staff members at the fort believe that Captain Kingsley still haunts the Officers' Quarters, although he hasn't been that active recently. He dislikes having his bed made. It takes a brave and understanding staffer to get the ghost to co-operate. Making his bed use to be a daily occurrence; but now it isn't so bad, according to the staff.

However, we can say that there was a strong presence there because someone followed us downstairs to the room below the Officers' Quarters and back upstairs to the Soldiers' Barracks. There was a window between the Captain's room and the Soldiers' Barracks. We looked back into the Captain's room. There were some deer antlers on top of the Captain's writing tables. Cathy said that the antlers didn't belong there. In fact, she could see a shako resting on top of the desk instead. Adam could also see the ghostly shako; plus a ghostly washing bowl which Cathy couldn't see.

I walked up to a female staffer and questioned her about the other ghosts at the fort. There had been a blonde haired, little girl with curls, who had been seen throughout the fort recently. The visitors to the fort always asked about her because she was wearing a Victorian style dress and they were wondering if she was a re-enactor.

Usually only the children visitors at the fort can see the ghostly children; but the blonde girl appeared to be upset for some reason. Perhaps that is why she was "more visible."

There was also a family group of ghosts in the kitchen area according to the staffer. The odd thing was that the women ghosts could only be seen by the male visitors to the fort. We were in the kitchen area while the staffer was taking a break and the usual camera tricks were taking place. Cathy noticed that one of the windows slowly shut on its own. There was no wind.

Cathy felt that some of the bones of the women and children were never found because they weren't buried with the soldiers. The women and children could have been blown up without a trace after the great explosion as well. Either way, they didn't associate themselves with the military burials.

The spookiest ghosts were the ones without arms, legs and heads. These were the soldiers who died in battle for the most part. When many of the bones of soldiers were discovered at Snake Hill and reburied in a proper manner, many of these spirits stopped showing up.

After leaving the fort, we went for a long walk and eventually made our way back to the car which was parked close to the fort. Adam looked into his bag and said that our car had been broken into. He claimed that someone had taken an adaptor apart, bent his book and put some sticky substance on Jacob's penny whistle. The adaptor end for the portable radio had the tape taken off. His book had indeed been bent in two and the penny whistle was sticky. However, all of the doors had been locked and there was no sign of forced entry. In other words, we had a spirit intruder.

Cathy stated that the last time Adam's book was marked; the spirit was trying to tell us something about the American troops who attacked Queenston Heights. This time it was American troops, who didn't like us being there. Our family had strong connections with the British side and not surprisingly, we had a similar problem with the American spirits at Lundy's Lane the year before. The worst was still ahead; since we were on our way to the battlefield at Chippewa.

The Battle of Chippewa

August 13, 2007

More than eight hundred men were killed, wounded or found to be missing as a result of this battle. We consider Chippewa to be the most haunted battlefield in Niagara. If you are looking for ghosts, your best bet is either Fort Mississauga or Chippewa after dark. Both of these sites are uninhabited and you can walk right onto the grounds any time you want to. But do you really want to? Maybe you had better read this first.

There were a few American tourists at the monument, but they left as it began to get dark. Dusk is the wrong time to visit this site, if you don't want to run into any ghosts.

Cathy had both of her digital cameras with her. The spirits not only prevented her from taking shots, they turned off both of the cameras. Every time she produced a camera, she would turn it on and the ghosts would turn it off. In spite of this cat and mouse game, Adam was able to take pictures most of the time without a problem.

We walked over several parts of the battlefield. Most of the battlefield appeared to be very "heavy" to the psychic. Cathy described it as being worse than Lundy's Lane. It was like someone was constantly shouting at her. There were only a few light areas where she noticed the warmth returning. Cathy and Adam both had headaches and felt rather poor throughout the visit, but we kept at it as long as possible. Cathy kept saying that the ghosts didn't want us to be there. She also thanked God that they didn't build on the battlefield, since they were going to do just that a few years before.

For some reason, I asked everyone to get off the path near the monument. At that point everyone could smell gunfire. Cathy was in terrible pain. Her fear of the unknown made her run back to the car. I gave the keys to the boys and stood my ground. Then I went back to the car and asked the boys to join me.

Jacob thought that the battle was just beginning. Both of the boys said that they could see flashes of uniforms and even the sound of muskets; but with the dusk, there were also sounds coming from the Niagara River and elsewhere. Both Adam and Jacob also sensed something happening in the trees on the other side of the darkening field.

When we got back to the car, Cathy was terrified. She had heard drums, fifes and marching going right past her. She had an incredible headache and she kept saying over and over that they didn't want her at Chippewa. She said that even though many more soldiers died at Lundy's Lane, the dead were more at peace there. In contrast, Chippewa was totally hostile. The bad feelings got worse as we left, until I got out the jet. I aimed the jet around the car until Cathy's arms started to tingle and she felt warm again. She said that she didn't like Chippewa and she would never return to the horror of it.

I felt that we still had a stowaway from either the fort or the battlefield, since there was a very strong smell in the car just after we arrived home. I ran for the tomahawk and the crystal power rod. Adam said that when he went upstairs to his room, he saw Jacob's door open and close. I confronted the ghostly intruder in Jacob's room and there were no other problems that evening.

Fort Niagara

August 15, 2007

Fort Niagara has been occupied by French, British and American soldiers. It's guaranteed that no two visits to Fort Niagara will be the same. We only had a few hours for this visit, so we went directly to the French Castle to begin our adventure with the supernatural.

I asked everyone to proceed to the top floor where I got my famous totem pole shot of several spirits last fall. Upon our arrival on the top floor, Jacob was poked on the 3rd chakra by a spirit and Adam had an interesting experience with a coaster.

Jacob bought an American oversized five cent coaster for Adam at the gift shop. Adam had put it near him as he sat down. It was flung away from him, to the floor by unseen hands. The coaster was heavy and the loud metallic clang startled all of us. There would be two more problems with this coaster before the day was done. I wasn't sure that the coaster was a good idea; but Jacob chose it for him and said that it would be okay.

Other difficulties occurred on the second floor. There was a smell like a latrine which followed us around. At least that was what I thought it was. Then I began to analyze the smell. Whereas human flesh smells sweet; this smell was like rotting flesh and death. It was so off-putting that I produced my jet pendant. I decided that I should remove the smell from the chapel. I also walked around on my own to see where the smells would lead me. There were pockets of it where the spirits were located. They were always close to us or nearby.

Cathy was overcome on the second floor and had to sit on a bench for five minutes before she could proceed downstairs and leave the building. She stated that the fort was entirely different from the last time we had visited. With hundreds of years of history to consider, it was not surprising.

After we left the French Castle, we came upon a gravestone less then one hundred feet from the castle. The gravestone indicated that there were unknown defenders buried beneath. Cathy said that many of the ghosts at the fort were in fact unknown defenders from the War of 1812.

Adam and Jacob sat right beside the gravestone and decided to play a game. Adam asked Jacob if he wanted heads or tails. Jacob said he wanted heads. Adam said that he could have heads, if that was his wish.

Adam did not throw the coaster into the air. Instead he brought it down on the cement. It kept vibrating on its rim; but it was clearly tails. Then the coin stopped. The instance that the coin stopped, it was heads. We've seen these spirit tricks before; but Adam couldn't believe his eyes. Adam re-stated that the coin was tails right up to the point where it stopped. He said that it was changed at the last possible moment.

Back in the car, we got ready to leave. As we pulled out of the parking lot, the entire car smelled of rotten flesh and death. I used the jet and everything smelled fresh again.

When we got home, Adam took his bag with the large nickel coaster into the house. He checked for the nickel coaster once he had the bag inside. The coaster was missing. I went around the house with the power rods and then I went outside to the car to look for the coaster with Adam. We didn't find anything and came back inside. Adam opened up his bag and found his nickel coaster. He claimed it wasn't there five minutes before.

Fort Erie

August 27, 2007

The action began as we arrived in the parking lot at Fort Erie. Cathy was getting her camera ready and she turned around and said something to me.

She said, "Get the gun from the pack."

The channeled message from the spirit was obviously from a soldier who thought that I should arm myself before proceeding into the fort.

Cathy mentioned that the psychic feelings around the fort changed on a constant basis. She had problems taking pictures as usual mainly because she was psychic. While she was in the Officers' Kitchen, she noted a spirit standing in the corner. She tried to take the picture and it wouldn't take. She watched as the spirit moved away and she was able to take the picture. As we moved to the Guard Room, she stated that the same ghost had followed her from one place to another.

I asked Adam to view the Officers' Quarters through the opening in the Soldiers' Barracks on the second floor. He saw the ghostly shako the same as before; only this time, the phantom image didn't last as long.

After we left the fort, Jacob was in the men's washroom by himself. He said that the door to one of the stalls shut by itself and then opened again. There was no wind and no one else around of course.

Fort Niagara

August 29, 2007

For ghost hunters, it's always a good day to visit Fort Niagara. This is one fort where the spirits like to swarm you. If you don't like close and personal, this place is not for you.

On the top floor, it was nasty at first. Cathy had a hard time adjusting. Both Adam and Cathy described the feeling as exactly what we experienced at Fort Mississauga. I could smell them all around me. After I used the jet, things settled down again. Cathy said that the fort was okay and that the spirits which were with us when we first arrived on the top floor were from Fort Mississauga.

As we stood by the stairs going down, Cathy quickly got out her camera and took a few pictures. Jacob thought he could smell a cigar. He also saw a white figure coming up the stairs from below and then going back down again, using another staircase. Cathy could sense the same figure in between the two staircases, so she took another picture before the spirit left.

Afterwards, we were sitting on the two benches near the North Redoubt. A boy and a girl had been inside the building. They were both about eight years old. The young girl came out first. Her father was waiting for the two children outside the building.

As she walked towards her father, she said, "Something strange happened. They put out the barrels; but when we looked back, they were gone." We began to investigate ourselves. Adam and Cathy both developed headaches while they were in the building. While the two children were on the top floor of the Redoubt, the barrels must have appeared. After we arrived on the top floor, Cathy became fearful and panic-stricken. She moved a few feet over to escape the psychic feelings of fear. As a result, she began to sense sadness instead.

After we left the building, Cathy explained. She said that when we arrived at the North Redoubt, a battle was going to take place. Cathy also felt "a sense of urgency" that was related to the powder barrels. Even though much of what happened in the North Redoubt was an emotional replay, she felt that most of the spirit activity at the fort was "real time."

Fort George Tunnel

July 26, 2009

On July 26, 2009, we experienced a few oddities in the tunnel. Because it was dark in the tunnel, there were a few lamps to help light the way. On this particular visit, everyone noticed a silhouette on the tunnel wall. It had the distinct shape of a shako. Just to make sure it was a shako, we checked for the silhouette on the way out of the tunnel. It had vanished.

Another unusual event took place on the same visit. Adam was wearing running shoes that day. As he went through the tunnel on the way to the octagonal blockhouse, nobody noticed anything amiss. But on the way back through the tunnel, everyone noted that Adam's running shoes sounded very loud; in fact, they sounded like the heavy leather boots of a marching soldier.

McFarlane House

July 26, 2009

The McFarlane House is just south of Fort George and a few hundred feet away from Niagara River. John McFarlane along with his sons built the home in 1800, after King George III granted him the land.

During the War of 1812 McFarlane House was used as a hospital by both the British and the American armies. It is one of the few buildings in the Niagara-on-the-Lake area to survive the War of 1812. By some miracle the building was not destroyed by the Americans, as they retreated from Fort George on December of 1813, after they burned down the entire town of Newark.

The Niagara Parks Commission restored the home in 1959. It was furnished in Empire style as representative of life as it was in Niagara, between 1800 and 1830.

We started walking up towards McFarlane House from Fort George a few years before, on a routine basis, so that Adam and Jacob could use the swings in the adjacent park while Cathy and I enjoyed the lovely surroundings.

The western sky was still bright, as we left the park beside McFarland House around 8:00 p.m. Adam was looking back at Jacob and telling him to hurry. He saw that both Cathy and I were beginning to walk back towards Fort George. In fact, we had already passed McFarlane's old house. Adam looked at the McFarlane House for a few seconds, but what he saw didn't register with him until he turned his head involuntarily towards Jacob's voice and then back again towards the McFarland House which was closed at the time.

Adam saw a ghost sitting on the front porch. The woman was about 25 years old, and she was dressed in an ankle length black dress with black boots or shoes. She had a white V neck. Her hair was blonde and it was parted in the middle. It was very tidy in a tight bun at the back of her head.

Adam also mentioned that the ghost was very sad. Adam was a little unsettled because she had looked right at him before he turned his head away and back again. Within seconds, she had vanished. There was a very large flowerpot in the same place where the ghost had been.

McFarlane House

August 5, 2009

We returned just over a week later so I could verify Adam's account. Adam spotted the spirit in the same place: at the side door, near a large flowerpot. The flowerpot was placed on a single slab of concrete beside a door which faced the Niagara River. There was only a slab of concrete leading from the door and a flowerpot; yet Adam claimed that the woman was sitting. As mentioned, the flowerpot never appeared when the woman was seen at the same time.

Adam was only able to track her for about two seconds at a time. She appeared to be capable of creating time slips as well. Whenever she was spotted, things would look the way they use to look. Within five seconds, Adam spotted the spirit again looking out from a bottom floor window on the other side of the house near the main entrance. Cathy could also track the ghost.

We sat in the front garden on a bench as Cathy gave me a blow-by-blow account where the ghost was moving throughout the house. Apparently, the ghost preferred the downstairs and wasn't very happy about something.

There also appeared to be a live human being upstairs. I believe we disturbed him and maybe we upset him because the curtains were drawn doing our investigations. Both Adam and Cathy thought the live person was a man. I wonder if he knew that he is sharing his home with a young female ghost.

McFarlane House

August 19, 2009

We returned to McFarlane House again on August 19, 2009. Adam noticed the ghost looking out the same window as before. Apparently, the ghost didn't interact with the person who was living in the home. They didn't appear to have much in common.

While we sat near McFarlane House, we noticed a man playing with his little girl on the swings. The man got a phone call and took the little girl off the swing for a minute. Adam began to play his fife. After the man was finished with his phone call, he asked if Adam wouldn't mind playing for his little girl. He did so.

The man and the little girl were over one hundred feet away. The little girl came over with a euro and gave the money to Adam. Cathy had spent half of her life in Europe. She said to me that the man was Dutch. He thanked us and we thanked him. Adam was impressed with the man's generosity since he wasn't expecting it. In the background, the ghost continued to look out the window at us. I asked Cathy why a spirit would want to stay lonely in a house for centuries. She told me that perhaps the spirit liked the house.

Cathy and I had just celebrated our wedding anniversary and I had not been able to provide her with an appropriate gift during our visit to Niagara-on-the-Lake. After arriving home, Cathy found a beautiful dress in her clothes closet. The spirits had provided the gift. The dress was a brand name and not something made up in the spirit world. When the spirits go shopping, they always get the right size too. She put it on for the rest of the evening.

The next morning, I thought about a picture of Jacob which was still being displayed over by the Fort George parking lot. Jacob's picture had been taken along with twenty other children in red coats on a special events day about four years ago. Like the picture, Jacob would treasure that day in time like so many other memories. I also believe that some ghosts want to retain their timeless memories too, regardless of the "illusions around them."

McFarlane House

August 25, 2009

Just before leaving home on our last summer journey to McFarlane House, both Cathy and I heard someone in the master bedroom washroom which was directly above the family room where we were talking. It sounded like a bit of commotion with a few of the cats as well. We went upstairs and discovered three of our cats staring at the washroom door with Sammy the cat being locked in the washroom. I distinctly heard human footsteps coming from the upstairs during the struggle, but no human had been upstairs in the washroom at the time. Sammy had been with us not a moment before, but he had the misfortune of being targeted by the negative entity. Since I had placed my British redcoat on the upstairs landing, the cats had been targeted on occasion. Nevertheless, the negative entities always knew when I was going to visit the forts and they always tried to disrupt my attempts to leave.

We left for the Niagara area later than usual, so that the sun was almost setting by the time we arrived at the McFarlane House. Cathy said that there were more spirits at the house this time. Adam said the same thing.

The spirits were also trying to communicate with Cathy. Cathy said that the original ghost that we had seen was from the Victorian era and not from the War of 1812. In fact, there didn't appear to be any spirits from the War of 1812 in the area. When we got home, Cathy had put her precious stone necklace down on her dressing room table before having a shower. When she went to get it, it had disappeared. She asked Adam if he would help her find it. Within a few minutes, she looked down and noticed that she was wearing it.

The good guys had put the necklace around her neck without her even being aware of it. She actually experienced a necklace being put around her neck over a year ago when no one was around. After Cathy got over the feeling of being a bit sheepish about the whole affair, she reminded me that the good guys work better when I visit the forts, regardless of the bad guys' nasty tricks.

McFarlane House

March 17, 2010

We always visited McFarlane House and Fort George when we are in Niagara-on-the-Lake. After the long and dreary winter, the house looked neglected and unloved. There were even pockets of negativity as you approached the house. Cathy stated that someone nasty was near her but had decided to go over to the house instead.

We sat on our favourite park bench while the boys took to the swings for twenty minutes or so. Cathy said to me that there was someone right behind her, but the spirit was friendly. I was looking at a memorial tag hanging from a tree branch. Cathy said that the bench also had a plaque on it. I read the plaque which was in loving memory of "_______." Cathy said that she got an incredible cold chill from that.

She said that not all of the spirits were earthbound and that some of them came back to sit on the bench and enjoy things as they did in the past.

Note (1): During later visits, we discovered that the psychic energy from the patio section at the back of the house was responsible for most of the nastiness. It appeared to extend outwards to the fringe of the cycle path so that intermittent negative energy could be picked up by those who are sensitive enough. Based on the description of the smell and feelings of what Cathy experienced in the fall of 2010, I believe that the back of the house (where the patio now exists) was where much suffering took place.

Note (2): Please note that I promised Cathy that I would not print the sensations and smells that she experienced which are related the McFarlane field hospital and to other battlefield conditions. If you are psychic and you are close to the house, the garden at the front is peaceful and very lovely (where the tourists go), but when you walk around to the back of the house, you might get hit with a wall of negativity.

Haunted Forts and Battlefields of 1837

The Battlefield at Prescott, Ontario August 8, 2007

The main action after the War of 1812 was the rebellion of 1837 which occurred in both Upper and Lower Canada. Troops from Fort Wellington were called out to attack a force which had landed downriver on the shores of the St. Lawrence River, at a place called Windmill Point. The Battle of the Windmill left 53 rebels dead and 17 British and loyal militia dead. The battle took place over four days and there were two bloody skirmishes before the rebels surrendered. Compared to most large scale battles, this one might look minor; but from a psychic's perspective that is not the case.

Upon arrival, we noted that the windmill was closed, so we weren't able to visit the building. The area around the building was fine. We didn't notice any psychic phenomena until we went down some stairs to the banks of the river.

Jacob went to the side of the river where he disturbed a large black snake. According to Jacob, it turned its head, hissed at him and disappeared under some foliage. It startled him a bit; since he was not use to finding large snakes slithering around his feet.

Cathy came down last and she was immediately hit by a "psychic blast" of immense proportions. She compared it to Fort Mississauga. Both Cathy and Adam had headaches from the time they reached the river bank. Cathy also felt dizzy and nauseated. Afterwards, Cathy said that most of the river bank appeared to be negative. The trail beside the river was especially bad; since it was the actual battlefield.

Cathy could only go up the trail about 15 paces before she had to turn around. I went up the trail myself and turned around and came back. She tried to take at least half a dozen pictures of me coming back towards her. The camera would not work. Once I stood right beside her, the camera "was allowed" to take a picture.

Fort Wellington

August 8, 2007

Fort Wellington was built to protect against enemy encroachment during the War of 1812 and the Rebellions of Upper Canada. Because of the age of the fort, one might expect to find at least one ghost.

The main blockhouse was composed of three floors. The supplies room with its barrels of rum, tea, and coffee was decidedly negative. The corridor which ran just outside the display room on the third floor was particularly negative.

The Caponniere at Fort Wellington projected into the south portion of the dry ditch. This defensive structure was made of thick stone, heavy timber and tin. It had rifle ports for the British defenders and a stone walled tunnel which provided a passageway to the structure. The tunnel was not as long as the one at Fort George; but tunnels by their very nature as dark passageways appear to attract psychic phenomena.

Fort Henry

August 9, 2007

Fort Henry was strong enough to defend itself from the American fleet during the War of 1812. However, the Americans never came. Fort Henry was also difficult to escape from, so it ended up serving as a prison during the Rebellion of 1837. All of the prisoners from the rebellion era ended up here on their way to the gallows, or to Australia.

We had been going to this fort for the past four years. There had been some unusual happenings on the ghost tour like doors closing by themselves or just slamming shut. The most haunted area in the old fort appeared to be near the Officers' Quarters. There were several glassed-in rooms full of antiques along a very dark hallway. Even when the sun was doing its best, it was very dark in the hallway because they kept the exit doors shut. It certainly added atmosphere to the place. I was "hiding" down the hallway from a small group of people when I heard one of them say that "it's gone because you were shouting at it."

Then I watched this woman go around the corner of a darkened wall and look in the corner at nothing. About five minutes later, I found Cathy in the school room which was just around the corner. I took her back with me to the Officers' Quarters and showed her the spot. She peeped around the corner and ran away saying that *it was still there*. There was an incident at the fort many years ago in which they had to hang someone at least four times, before they could finally say it was a done deal. Perhaps the ghost that was hiding in the Officers' Quarters was still trying to evade the noose.

There was also an incident of a knife which disappeared from the cooking area and showed up in different parts of the fort, until the fort's administration decided to remove it. On another occasion, some construction work in the old fort made some of the spirits restless. One of the fort's spirits got angry and started "breaking glass" without the benefit of real glass of course. However, the sound of glass breaking was real enough that the security guards called in the police a couple of times. Even the police heard the breaking of glass; but after searching for hours, no one was ever found.

Another interesting spectre use to walk around in rags. Nothing upsets the Fort Henry Guard more than a disorderly ghostly soldier who doesn't listen.

Adam and Jacob also claimed that they had seen white shapes and shadows in the reverse firing chamber and in other parts of the fort. During the summer of 2008, Adam and Jacob decided to investigate the reverse firing chamber after making sure that no other tourists were present. Apparently, it didn't make any difference whether the boys were alone or together; they both swore that they could see the white shape of a soldier, on each of their journeys below the main floor. Moreover, they both claimed that the same ghost had followed them down into the reserve firing chamber and back up again, on previous visits to the fort.

Fort Henry

August 28, 2008

The following paranormal incident at Fort Henry comes from the book Shadow People (2009). This incident suggests that sometimes people can be the "source of the problem."

We had been visiting the fort for the past six years and the fort normally closes at 5:00 p.m. However, today the fort was allowed to be left open until 8:00 p.m. Therefore, we decided to stay later than usual.

We were observing the big guns when a young boy started to "bad mouth" the fort, since he felt it was "pointless." Then, he started to kick the 24 pound cannons and make additional negative comments.

Cathy was nearby and she got slapped for no reason. Then both Adam and Jacob witnessed the naughty boy being pushed down a set of stairs by some angry spirits.

Cathy was really fed up with it all, since she would not have been hit herself, except for the irritable, bad-mannered little boy. She left the area immediately. Then both Adam and Jacob witnessed the little boy's older brother hit the little boy because he had still "not learned to behave."

If you are a seasoned ghost tracker, you can draw your own conclusions. For example: the issue of respect towards the spirits, being the innocent bystander and being at a particular place, at the wrong time. Moreover, if you look at the situation from the ghosts' point of view, perhaps they were a little disturbed by the change in schedule.

Re-enactment Weekend at Fort George

Scouting for Ghosts

Being part of the scout movement provides excellent opportunities to gather information on battlefield ghosts. The 2007 re-enactment of the War of 1812 at Fort George was no exception. The identity of the following venture scout has been changed to protect my source.

Upon arriving at the 1812 re-enactor camp at Fort George, a chance encounter with a ventures scout lead to me to believe that Fort York in Toronto was much more haunted than I thought previously. The scout was staying a few nights in a Fort York blockhouse which is usually reserved for staff. It's located right beside the archaeology museum. It wouldn't surprise me that some of the recent digging at the fort had something to do with the haunting. This is also one of the scariest ghost story that I've heard from someone other than my own.

This ghostly event took place at 2:00 in the morning. Peter was sleeping near the top of the stairs with his troop when he was awoken by the thumping of someone or something coming up the steps. Peter could feel the hair on the back of his head stand on end as he witnessed a sight that few people ever see. He saw an apparition ascending the top part of the staircase. The ghost was a woman. Her appearance was a classic white one except for two unsettling features. The first one was the tray. Peter said that he could tell that she was holding onto a silver tray. The second item was more gruesome. She had something like a musket ball wound right in the middle of her forehead. Peter could also make out the colour of the wound as pink, not bright red. Peter was almost at his wits end, as the ghost reached the top of the stairs right by his bed. However, as the phantom reached the top floor, it disappeared.

Even though many of the scouts were awakened by the sound of the footsteps, no one else saw the ghost except for Peter. Peter added that most of the other scouts would have had a problem viewing the phantom on the stairs from where they were sleeping anyway.

If that wasn't bad enough, the entire event took place again the next night. Only this time it happened earlier. Peter couldn't be exact about the time, but he claimed it was at least fifteen minutes before two. It could even have been a half an hour earlier.

This time everyone heard the thumping coming up the staircase. Peter woke up with a feeling of dread. He felt that he would never sleep again, if he had to face the gruesome phantom one more time. The ghost finally got to the top of the stairs the same as before and then it stopped. Luck was with him; the ghost did not materialize.

Peter offered his own interpretation of this event. He felt that the ghost was a nurse of sorts and that she had been killed on active duty. Whether that's true or not, perhaps the ghost still thinks that it's helping someone in the blockhouse.

Ghost Tour at Fort George

As part of our 1812 re-enactment weekend, Adam and I went on the ghost tour with the same guide who saw the phantom of an American soldier in the tunnel on a previous visit. Our appointed guide had been nervous in the past, but now he seemed more confident. Still he was warning us not to tell him anything about any ghosts that we might see on the tour. Our guide had been in a support role to other tour guides and now he was hitting his stride. So I decided not to ruin his day by spilling the beans.

The tour started off in blockhouse one. It was perfectly quiet except for what sounded like a party. Adam heard the same party everywhere in the fort except for the tunnel. He strongly felt that the ghostly party was being held in the Officers' Quarters. Unfortunately, we never got there because a family of skunks decided to spoil our entrance. We had to exit the fort prematurely; but not before visiting the tunnel.

Some visitors to the fort have witnessed soldiers emerging from diabolical black mists within the tunnel. I don't disagree with that story. In fact, I would go one step further and say that the tunnel itself is an evil place.

We already knew the tunnel routine. I suggested to Adam that we go into the tunnel last. We didn't go all the way in, and we kept back a bit, so we could see the tunnel entrance clearly.

We also knew that our guide would trick people into following him in with the lantern. Then he would turn the tables. After a few spine-tingling stories, he would race towards the tunnel exit and steal the light from all of those who went into the tunnel first. On this particular night, two things happened in the tunnel. The first one was right out of Edgar Allen Poe. Adam put his hand on the tunnel wall and it had a heartbeat. Was the tunnel a spirit or was there a ghost right beside him attached to the tunnel? More than likely it was one or the other.

We had been told a few stories about the tunnel opening, but Adam saw something different. Instead of the little girl, who sometimes comes out to observe the ghost tour, there was a shadow at the entrance. Then for about five seconds there was an evil face; the stuff of nightmares.

Some of the fort visitors might be getting bored of the Watcher story. Some of them claim that the Watcher isn't really that scary from a distance while others are still terrified of what is considered the most frightful ghost in the fort. Perhaps there is more than one Watcher. If so, does he watch the tunnel when the tourists go in? Apparently, this Watcher also has an evil grin. Personally, I could think of better places to be, if I was a tour guide and I had to deal with it.

Re-enacting as Medicine

Historical forts are on hallowed ground. Battlefield areas also have a special spiritual significance attached to them. Many spirits walk where the dead have fallen.

In general, re-enacting creates positive energy. A play or a concert depends on the audience; but a re-enactment of a historical event is totally dependent on the re-enactors. It makes no difference whether there are different uniforms on the battlefield, opposed or otherwise. Weather conditions are not a factor either. The only requirement is that the re-enactment of a historical event should be perceived as a tribute to those who have lived before. Only then can any healing power be created.

* * *

Of course, there is always the negative side of human emotions which create psychic imprints on the land. For example, the psychic imprints of Fort Niagara and its previous military battles can be observed from both Fort Mississauga and Fort George.

In some cases, human spirits still stand on guard. Fort Mississauga was abandoned by the military many years ago and that could be part of the problem. If you walk around the outside walls of the fort, everything will appear normal. However, if you're psychic and you venture inside the fort's walls, you may sense negativity being directed towards you. The same can be said about battlefields which have been turned into monuments. Queenston Heights and Chippewa are both good examples of how psychic phenomena can turn negative at times.

In brief, regardless of how historical forts or battlefields appear to you, there's always a chance that you'll run into an unpleasant surprise in a dark tunnel.

The Spirit Warriors of Fort Mississauga and Fort George

On this particular day in May of 2008, we had been visiting Niagara-on-the-Lake. We had hiked around Fort George and we had walked up to Fort Mississauga. We saw at least a dozen young people go into Fort Mississauga; but I refused to go into the fort because of the problems we had experienced there the year before.

We didn't notice anything as we walked away from the fort and back to the car. However on hindsight, one can easily conclude from this incident and from other visits to the forts that the spirits of soldiers are allowed to leave their posts, under the right circumstances. I now believe it's possible that we've carried spirits from the fort, on just about every occasion we've been in Niagara. The spirits usually return to the fort from our car or from our home, after a short stay. I also believe that most spirits who do leave the forts do not intend to cause problems. In fact, I believe that they have protected us from evil spirits on many occasions.

Normally Cathy gets a forlorn feeling of sadness when she leaves the Niagara area. On this particular trip homeward, Cathy, Jacob and Adam all felt extremely sad, as we passed Stoney Creek on the Queen Elizabeth Expressway. Stoney Creek is where the Americans were halted by British regulars, after the May 1813 invasion which destroyed both Point Mississauga and Fort

George. Usually, we reach Burlington before the psychic feelings of forlorn sadness begin. But as we drive away from both Burlington and Lake Ontario, the feelings of sadness begin to disappear. Cathy believes that this particular psychic phenomenon is caused by the soldier spirits who have not gone beyond Burlington during their lifetimes and must return to their fort. In other cases, the spirits have something in common with us from a previous lifetime, or there is a personal interest which allows them to break free of their geographic confinements. These spirits are able to return home with us.

Adam usually plays military march music on the way home from the forts. On this trip, we had put on the radio and the radio hosts were playing some mellow classical music. We would have saved ourselves some bother if we had played *British Grenadiers* instead.

By the time we got home, Cathy was feeling extremely cold. It didn't look good; so I asked Adam and Jacob to help me out.

It was Jacob who captured the first lot of them with the commander. He knew exactly when it happened because the crystal power rod which he was holding became very warm all of a sudden. I knew we didn't have them all; but I told Jacob to follow me outside. Jacob told me that we must transfer the spirits from his power rod into mine before we went outside because they were too powerful. That should have been my first clue.

After we arrived at the back of the house, Jacob asked me where I wanted to send them. He suggested that it should not be any place in our local neighbourhood. I told him that I wanted them to be sent to Fort Mississauga. We both visualized Fort Mississauga and sent them on their way.

Jacob and I rushed back inside the house, where both Cathy and Adam were dealing with the remaining spirits. I started to do another monologue about sending the spirits back to Fort Mississauga, but Cathy told me to stop what I was doing. She stated what we needed to do instead. We had to play *British Grenadiers* on the stereo and then the soldiers would go back. She was in tears as she told me that quite a few British soldiers from the Niagara area had followed us home. However, all the soldiers who had followed us needed orders. Jacob had picked up the same message from the commander, who had just returned from Fort Mississauga. Moreover, Cathy stated that she was getting visions of soldiers leaving England before their arrival in Upper Canada, after seeing action in Spain during the Napoleonic Wars. She could also make out the uniform details of the soldiers. These soldiers appeared to be dressed in grey trousers, rather than the standard white ones.

The commander was still a bit angry; but he settled down after Adam played *British Grenadiers.* However, Adam played the orchestrated version and the commander told us that it did not have enough power to send them back to their fort. Adam got out his copy of some Fort George musicians who played the drums and fifes the old way. He played about ten or fifteen seconds of it. All of the spirits were returned to their fort, as a result of the music. It was quite an event. Although I sat rather stiff faced through the proceedings, the ordeal of the soldiers moved me. Cathy reminded me that releasing the soldiers from their earthbound status of guarding their fort could create a void with unforeseen consequences. I agreed with her. Although it goes against common wisdom, some theories of the earthbound appear to me to be too simplistic. In fact, I believe that Fort George is connected to a higher spiritual centre. I also believe that the forts in general are all in need of earthly healing power from human beings and that needs to be taken into consideration as well.

Spirit Warriors

I have always regretted sending a small company of soldiers back to Fort Mississauga before I had a chance to understand why they came with us in the first place. With that incident in mind, we set off for Fort George on March 17th, 2010. A good part of the fort was being repaired for the 1812 bicentennial anniversary. There were a couple of unsightly roads going up to the fort and a huge crane. There was a vast amount of lumber and sections of the fort lying around everywhere. I knew that the spirits would not be happy with the renovations.

We walked up to McFarlane House and back to the fort again. The display pictures near the fort's front entrance held the memories of a special events day that now seemed so long ago. One of the pictures showed Jacob and about twenty other children in redcoats. Jacob was only eight years old when the picture was taken. Now he was a teenager.

We arrived back home. After I went inside the house, a few things started to happen right away. A spirit shoved the car door back on Cathy's foot. At the same time, Adam was taking a picture of Jacob in the back seat of the car when he saw a shadow go across his picture viewfinder. Jacob heard Adam say that a shadow had gone in front of the camera, but Adam didn't actually say it. It was intended as a warning.

Cathy came into the house in pain, followed by the others. After everyone was inside the house, Adam got both himself and Jacob some milk in a glass.

When Adam put the glass of milk in front of Jacob, Jacob heard Adam say "water." It was quite evident by then that there were two types of spirits present. There were shadow spirits and there were others.

I went around the house and cleared out the shadow spirits. While I was doing that a jacket was thrown at Cathy. When Cathy went to say something to Jacob about the coat, something totally different came out.

"My throat's been cut."

By that time, I was back in the front room with the three of them. The television had been turned on previous to the "coat throwing" incident, since we were about to watch a movie. But now there was a very strong odour of feet and an unusual red line at the top of the television screen. The spirits had given us the clues that we needed to identify them.

Cathy said, "Foot soldiers" and I said, "The thin red line."

The spirits of British Army regulars from the War of 1812 were now in my living room. This might have been the opportunity that I had waited for, but it turned out a bit different from what I expected. First of all I explained to the spirit warriors that the work on the fort was needed so that people would continue to come to the fort to honour the military traditions of the past. I also mentioned how I had done the same throughout my home. I asked them if there was anything I could do for them or whether they had anything to ask of me.

Cathy said that there was an incredible amount of sadness present. She said that I would have to promise to visit the fort more often. I was needed. I agreed to it and asked the commander if he needed any extra power to get back to the fort (traditional fife music would have done it). Cathy said that it wasn't necessary this time.

Many of the earthbound soldiers and other soldier spirits are in fact performing a valuable duty on the earth plane. In fact, they can't be sent to the light just yet. Some forts like Fort George are hubs of power for the soldiers in their mission to combat evil in certain situations. Some soldiers are able to visit me from various places and some battlefield spirits are free to travel in an unlimited fashion. I believe there are specific British Army regiments from the Napoleonic Wars, the French Indian Wars and the War of 1812 who are fighting a different kind of foe in the spirit world.

I was given the "final clue" on March 19th. One of our toy soldiers located in a barrister bookcase, who was holding the King's colours was knocked flat on its back. This timing was perfect. At that moment, I knew beyond a doubt that the British Army was involved. I don't know everything about their particular role in all of this "balancing out of things," but I do know that most of the fort's soldiers are aware of my movements in and around the fort.

After I return home from each trip to Fort George, I now sit in a chair with Cathy across the room. I give the troops the latest on the fort and Cathy gets a cold shudder from the conversation. I never ask the troops what I can do for them because that creates a great deal of sadness. Instead, I always promise them that I will be visiting the fort again soon. After I do that there is a moment of warmth and they go back to their fort without any further help from me.

* * *

It was drum and fife day at Fort George and the musicians were ramping up for the bicentennial. We arrived later in the day and because of some family difficulties, I almost decided not to go.

We visited inside the fort and talked with some of the re-enactors. Later on, we visited the octagonal blockhouse which had lost all of its negativity for some reason. Adam took a picture of me and discovered a bright light instead. I told him to take another picture. This time the light took up about 75% of picture.

Cathy said that there was a spirit standing beside me. Obviously, it was a high-level spirit because of the light and the lack of negativity in the blockhouse.

Later in the evening, we listened to some fife music while we were parked outside of the fort. I spoke with the spirits after we arrived home as usual. The representative of the fort was concerned. After I had committed myself to being present at the fort, I was thinking of canceling our visit earlier in the day. I apologized and explained.

I also stated that, "I would continue to bring light to the fort."

Cathy heard sometime different. The spirit told her that I would be "Enlightening the Fathers of the fort."

The fort's representative also wanted a firm commitment, concerning when I would be visiting again. I already had the date in mind. However, because I had created some concern in the ranks, Cathy gave me the exact words to say. I repeated her words, so that there would be no misunderstanding.

Afterwards, I thanked the fort's representative. The representative also stated that if I needed the soldiers for any reason, they would come instantly.

Note (I); The British Army was at its peak during the time of Napoleon so they would be an ideal force to deal with evil in areas which they once controlled. I also believe that Native American warriors act as protective guardians in league with the British Army in the Niagara area and areas further a field. In addition, the forts are needed as "spiritual hubs." Fort George is the "king pin" for the other satellite forts. All the artifacts of war and re-enactments which honour the dead help to rally those living (or otherwise), who need to both celebrate and heal their past selves. Accordingly, the living can learn valuable lessons without bloodshed.

Note (2): Even though Cathy has blocked most of her communicative ability with the spirits, she is able to channel brief messages from battlefield spirits like she did in the parking lot at Fort Erie when she told me "to bring my gun to the fort."

Note (3): My "emotional connection" with the forts began with my first visit over ten years ago. Once the spirits identified me, I had to keep up appearances. The Senior Council of Elders suggested that I visit as many of the forts as possible each year. Apparently, there are things on the earth plane which only humans can do. In particular, energy from our past lives has healing power for the spirits; therefore, it's important that "linked or shared energies" from both the present and the past are in harmony (notwithstanding the fact that everything in the spirit world is in the now, where past and present are perceived as one).

Note (4): Enlightening the Fathers of the fort refers to balancing energies at the fort. Please refer to the "Afterword and the Appendices."

Note (5): Jacob mentioned to me that spirits will not likely speak when there are too many people around; since a large group of people visiting a fort at the same time, actually creates a force field. The best time to experience paranormal phenomena is when the crowds back off a bit. However, when things do happen, there are usually few witnesses and sometimes a lack of awareness on the part of the "ghost hunters."

Fort George

Oct 23, 2010

October at the fort was particularly unusual this year.

We arrived too late at Fort George to pay the entrance fee (in my mind, if you arrive after four o'clock, it's too late to pay the entrance fee, given that they close the gates at five o'clock). Before we even approached the front gates of the fort, Cathy tried to take pictures of the boys, but a white "blob" kept getting in the way of the camera. She tried to take a few more pictures outside of the fort, but the spirits were having a bit of fun with her. In fact, they were probably trying to delay us for a few minutes.

The re-enactor soldier at the gate was the same fellow as the one who hosted the ghost tour many years ago when Adam spotted the American spirit on the staircase leading to the octagonal blockhouse. It was 4:15 p.m. and the fort was going to close at 5:00 p.m, but the re-enactor soldier was sending us to the office to get a family ticket. We didn't argue with him about getting the ticket. Instead, we chimed in resolute agreement with him.

We turned away from the gate and when I knew that the re-enactor soldier couldn't hear me, I said that we would walk into town instead of visiting the fort because it was too late to pay. As soon, as the words came out of my mouth, the soldier shouted out after us that we were to be admitted to the fort.

This change of mind happened so suddenly that we wondered if he had been persuaded to let us in by way of "spirit intervention."

We asked the re-enactor soldier how the ghost tours had been going.

The soldier answered, "The tours sold out well in advance."

He appeared to be in good humour because he was leading a tour that very night which he claimed that he didn't mind doing, *now that he had seen at least three ghosts.* Hurray! This was the same re-enactor who was afraid of his own shadow and had stopped doing ghost tours for years because of some fear. He must have jumped from category two, to category three (see below).

For arguments sake, let's say that there at least three types of people in the world who may have seen ghosts. Those who:

I. don't believe in ghosts (and are not interested in seeing them either)

II. have seen a ghost (but don't want to believe in them)

III. believe in ghosts (because the existence of ghosts doesn't challenge their belief system)

There was another woman near us who overheard our conversation. She was very amused by the announcement that there might be "real ghosts at the fort." She kept smiling the whole time, but I could tell that she thought that the whole thing was really a spin on Halloween. In spite of the woman's reluctance to embrace the re-enactor's admission, there was plenty of spirit activity in October which was hiding behind the bicentennial re-construction project at the fort.

* * *

We went directly to the octagonal blockhouse which is an interesting building from a paranormal point of view. The tunnel is a negative place, and the octagonal blockhouse is attached to it. There were tricks with the camera in which Jacob claimed that the faces that he saw in the viewfinder made the pictures look more evil in appearance. It's possible that the view finder could look evil and for the picture to look normal. Based on my experiences with paranormal, anything is possible. There were also similar incidents with the camera not working, or the unseen getting in the way of the lens. Cathy had her traditional psychic headache until she left the blockhouse and the tunnel. The moment she stepped out of the tunnel, everything was fine with the rest of the fort.

The most interesting incident which happened to us was when Cathy was coming down the stairs from the octagonal blockhouse towards the tunnel. She needed assistance because she lost contact with "where she was." She knew she was coming down the steps, but everything that she knew that was in front of her suddenly disappeared. Instead, she could see another dimension which was related to the spirits around her. The whole time she had a sense of unreality about what was happening to her.

While this "extra-dimensional" experience was going on in the tunnel, I was moving to the south-west palisade. I hopped up onto the outside wall and looked down on the octagonal blockhouse. I felt very proud of the fort. Although the spirits were having difficulties with the changes, the Canadian government had finally done something about the poor state of repairs.

* * *

After visiting downtown Niagara-on-the-Lake, we went for a walk to McFarlane House. It was getting dark and it was raining. We didn't meet one person on the pathway for the whole journey. On the way, Cathy spotted a shadow figure along the path which looked like a soldier with a cape. She got a very creepy feeling from that, so she was glad that it was even darker on the way back.

As we approached McFarlane House, Cathy experienced the "tunnel problem" all over again. It was a mist and it appeared to be engulfing the path in front of us. She lost her bearings and appeared to be in another place. She was not able to determine where she was.

I knew that no one was around, and no one would see me, so I exorcized whatever was on the path. After I used some techniques which I've developed over the years, the path in front of us cleared up and we were able to continue.

The boys had raced ahead of us and had cut over a bridge before they got to the part of McFarlane House which has been a problem for us on previous visits. Both Adam and Jacob said the same thing, about the negative side of MacFarlane House where the path curves. We strongly felt that the bicycle accident which took place in the same spot last summer in which an old man had to be evacuated by ambulance was no accident. The injured man actually believed that he was going too fast in order to rationalize his mishap. We knew better.

Note: Jacob had his scooter with him and tried to use it on the pathway, but felt that someone had put a brick in front of it, so that he went face forward and landed on his chest. Jacob picked himself up without any difficulty. At least Jacob understood that it was not entirely his own fault;

* * *

When we got home from our trip, we discovered a signal whistle and some bicentennial medals which had been placed in the house, but had been removed from the house and stored in the car's glove compartment instead.

We proceeded to go into our home. As per usual, we contacted the soldiers of the fort, who told us that "we were unified." The conversation had to do with my fort (how protecting my home was also good for the fort) and about visiting Fort George again in November.

There were always two parties which we had communicated with after our trips to Fort George. One spirit contact was through Cathy and the other was through Jacob. The authoritarian spirit which spoke through Jacob sounded like a commander, but something else happened this time. Jacob experienced a tunnel vision while talking with the "commander." A voice came through the tunnel (from a higher realm) and stated that I should *counter* the celebration of evil in October *by participating.*

The "October message" from the higher realms went further:

> ***I shouldn't ignore evil at Halloween; but I should counter its influence by turning the celebration of evil into something more positive.***

The aspect of the tunnel and the voice from the higher realms convinced me that Halloween should not be ignored.

* * *

The spirit or spirits who spoke through Cathy appeared to be related to the ones who showed sadness whenever we left the Niagara area for home. Their presence allowed Cathy to consider our defenses against the "others," in particular our home's vulnerable areas. We had just planted some trees in the backyard recently, but our defenses were just a bit weak on the "high school side of our home (the north side)." We moved a crystal cluster to the corner of the house which faced the high school and decided to hang a few more crystals to help reduce incidents.

Note (1): I had been taking it easy throughout most of the summer; however, autumn is when the negative energy in the community begins to build.

Note (2): The subject of the book *Shadow Place* was about our challenges with the "others" (referred to as "others" by the soldier spirits).

* * *

Our November trip took place only two weeks after out Halloween trip. The boys had been involved with the Remember Day parade in the morning, but we were able to make our way to Niagara in the afternoon.

We had less than half an hour at Fort George this time. An older man at the gate let us into the fort. He was wearing a long grey overcoat. His large grey officer's hat was particularly striking. In fact, he was a dead ringer for the fort's surgeon.

I asked everyone to make for the southern octagonal blockhouse. There was a guardian spirit on the second floor and as a result, there were no incidents this time. I read a tribute to the British Grenadiers which the spirits themselves wrote for me many years ago.

This letter was left on my desk many years ago.

British Grenadiers

Soldiers fight;

But we are more,

We're the British Grenadiers.

Oh, we're the boys;

Who feared no noise,

We're the British Grenadiers.

God save the King and heaven bless:

The soldiers of their country.

Oh yes, we are red coated and gold,

We're the British Grenadiers.

We left the fort and I escorted Cathy, Jacob and Adam into town. I returned to the closed fort on my own and made my way to a "blind spot" on the fort's palisade. The re-construction team should have used older wood in some cases. The vibrations of the new wood had caused a great deal of fear at the fort.

Nevertheless, I blessed the fort's energy and asked that both the living and the non-living be protected by the light.

* * *

As expected, we noted fear from the spirits on the way home, in addition to sadness. After arriving home, Jacob indicated to me that we would have to visit again in December before Christmas because of the bitterness that many of the soldiers felt at that time of year. It would appear that for many of them, peace and goodwill didn't exist in the way that it should have. Jacob reminded me that in addition to the re-construction problem, there would be less people visiting the fort

Besides the usual concerns, the Fathers of the fort communicated to me through Cathy that they were proud of me for attending in November. That's when "the others" began to eavesdrop. The negative spirits had actually set up their operations in my neighbour's home next door. Because I was being blocked by negative energy from one of my "neighbours," I decided to go through my house with three Atlantean power rods in one hand and the tomahawk in the other. I charged all of the crystals in the house until I gave Cathy a headache. I was being a bit more aggressive than usual because I wanted to hear more of what the spirits had to say. Jacob stated that "the others" were operating from our neighbour's home because it was unprotected. They were also enjoying what I had decided to do. If they could succeed in creating more aggression, they could gain energy from it. Jacob stated that by holding my tomahawk blade at my neighbour's house, I would eventually give him nightmares. I had heard enough. I put two of the power rods down and relaxed in a chair. Being aggressive was not the answer.

Even though Jacob could hear the voices trying to break through, the spirits were being blocked by "the others" in the house next to me. It was extremely frustrating. Nevertheless, Jacob reminded me that the power that I had was only to be used in defense and not in an aggressive manner. The lesson was that I had no right to interfere in my neighbour's affairs, so that I could access what I wanted. If I continued with my aggressive strategy, it would backfire. The lesson of interference is something that warmongering politicians need to adhere to as well, since evil gains strength from aggression.

A few days later, I contacted the Fathers of the fort. Their message was the same. Evil uses human disharmony and anger to further its cause. The spirits appeared to be worried that in our fight with evil, we should maintain harmony. They assured me that aggression against evil is not an option because it is too dangerous.

Jacob also reminded me that I wasn't to know too much, until the time was right because of the danger. He added that there were higher level spirits involved, including the "Admiral." Apparently, everyone in the spirit world calls Nelson, the "Admiral." I was surprised that Jacob didn't say anything about him before. In addition, I was curious about one of the generals that he had been talking with, but that is also a mystery for the time being.

Note (1): The involvement of higher level spirits raises more questions than answers. We have some knowledge about what happens in the afterlife and we know that Fort George has something to do with our karma, but many things still need to happen before we can reveal more layers of our truth.

Note (2): From our point of view, those who have dealt with dangerous entities have never had all of the answers. Unfortunately, people who refuse to allow themselves to believe in anything beyond their own experiences and their own beliefs can never know the true nature of "the others." Nor can they fathom the multi-layered aspects of human evil; in particular, that which is related to the negative energies of the spirit world.

Explaining the Inexplicable

With the advent of so-called new age thinking and "higher vibrations" there is a sense that visitors to haunted forts and battlefields have the ability to send earthbound soldiers to the light. However, there could still be some unresolved paranormal issues related to individual circumstances at haunted sites which could impact visitors. I've identified at least five different categories for those who are sensitive to the paranormal.

There are wheels within wheels, and dimensions within dimensions. For example, I was told that an unknown woman and her daughter were blown up at Fort George. Both of them were trapped in a fourth dimensional time warp. They were not fifty feet from each other in their spirit existence; yet, neither one of them was aware of the other's fate. I wasn't able to verify this information, but I do believe that time warps exist within different dimensions.

Somewhat related to time warps are time loops. Some situations create conditions where a limited number of souls on a battlefield are released to the light, whereas the rest must remain.

Much of the fourth dimension is also dependent on one's personal beliefs. If a spirit believes it is still alive as a human being, or experiencing a personal crisis, then that spirit will continue to act out its little drama. If the spirit had expanded its consciousness; let go of the earth plane; and accepted the higher vibrations associated with the light in the first place, then that spirit may have proceeded to a higher dimension on its own without any help. Perhaps that is the reason that the *light may only appear* for those who believe it is the true way to a higher existence. That is not to say that some spirits are denied. Rather it comes down to a perception of one's ego fears which could create further challenges.

In addition, spirits who have been affected by human evil or violence; do not necessarily go to the light. Sometimes a spirit is confused or disoriented because of sudden death; or there is too much anger, or emotion from human conflict. Under these adverse conditions, spirit guides are needed to help the disoriented to cross over.

Replays and psychic impressions also have to be considered. Powerful negative vibrations, in places of battle and bloodshed are absorbed on the earth plane. So it may take more than a few centuries to replace those vibrations with positive ones, even if effective healing strategies are employed.

Even though some paranormal activities may seem rather bizarre, there are still rules in our universe which regulate spirit activities. Free will is only half of the answer. Energy returned and balance will always be on the other side of the equation. Moreover, some aspects of the paranormal are kept secret; so we can't always put the whole picture together; or make perfect sense of what others say when it comes to interpreting our own experiences. Nevertheless, if you pay more attention to what you consider to be insignificant; then you might be better prepared to interpret the different varieties of paranormal phenomena which others have ignored. Don't forget that truth is often stranger than fiction, regardless of outcome. In addition, no matter how scientific a paranormal investigator claims to be, let it be known that some ghost hunters have experienced paranormal phenomena that is simply indescribable.

Note: The relationship between mankind and the earthbound has never been explained to me in a satisfactory manner. Many "new age" accounts say that the earthbound spirits need to go to the light. Nevertheless, I would suggest that paranormal researchers also consider the multi-dimensional aspects of the earthbound.

Illustrations of Forts and Battlefields

Barrels stored in Fort Henry

Brock's monument

Cannon in parade ground (Fort Henry)

Chippewa

Cottage (Fort George)

Fort George

Dundurn Castle

Dundurn Castle (side)

Entry (Fort Erie)

Fireplace (Fort York)

Fort Amherstburg

Fort Wellington

Fort George

Fort George armory

Fort George blockhouse

Fort George blockhouse and junior officers' quarters

Fort Henry

Fort Henry

Fort Henry entryway

Fort Henry upper

Fort Mississauga

Fort Mississauga front

Fort Mississauga tunnel

Fort Niagara doorway

Fort Niagara gateway

Fort Niagara (French Castle)

Fort Niagara tower

Fort York

Fort York landscape

Fort George tunnel

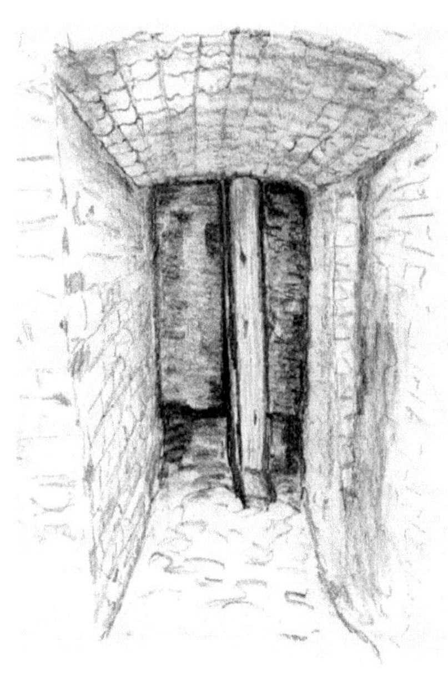

Fort Mississauga reverse room

Gage House (Stoney Creek)

Gated door (Fort Henry)

Gate (Fort Mississauga)

Gateway (Fort York)

Grandfather clock

Grenadiers

Hanlan’s Point lighthouse (near Fort York)

Junior officers' quarters (Fort George)

Kitchen (Fort York)

Laura Secord's home

Fort George lock up

Native American spirit (Fort Mississauga) by Cathy

Martello tower (Kingston)

McFarlane House

McFarlane House (frontage)

Monument (Lundy's Lane)

Navy Hall (near Fort George)

Octagonal blockhouse (Fort George)

Old Fort Niagara

Outer Fort Erie

Parade ground (Fort Henry)

Fort Wellington

Queenston Heights

Marks Angelican Church

Staircase (Fort Henry)

Tower (Stoney Creek)

Shako (circa 1812)

Upper parade (Fort Henry)

Windmill lighthouse (Prescott)

Part Two

Paranormal Phenomena at Home related to the War of 1812

Haunted places and paranormal activities at home can overlap. This section covers paranormal activities at home related to historical timelines, inanimate objects, telepathy, visual incantations, possession, spirit writing, psychic feedback from pictures on the internet, visualizing images from the spirit world, spirit music, elements which manifest from haunted places, channeling, aura fields, symbols and ghostly companions.

Spirit Telepathy

Most media attention (and paranormal literature) is focused on possession as the worst case scenario. There is no disputing the fact that demonic possession can be extremely dangerous. On the other hand, the use of telepathy by spirits can involve everything from sending visual messages, to assuming someone's shape and form (in the eye of the beholder of course). Accordingly, telepathy can be challenging to your mental health if you are not prepared for it. In other words, don't assume that people will take you seriously.

The Oxford English Dictionary defines telepathy as: "The communication of impressions from one mind to another, independently of the recognized channels of sense."

Telepathy can be conveyed by either deliberate efforts, or by dreams. In fact, telepathic dreams can leave an "impression" on more than one person.

Some spirits have the ability to use telepathy, and that should not be overlooked when you are communicating with the spirit realms.

Note: Native Americans are considered to be good spirit guides because of their sense of oneness with the universe. While on the earth plane, Native Americans walk the red road by going into the silence on vision quests.

This strategy is also considered to be an effective way of communicating with the divine.

Visual Incantations

Most people don't think that pictures or images can involve paranormal phenomena. However, Cathy, Jacob and Adam have all received negative psychic feedback on the internet from observing homes where murders have been committed. Read the following and decide for yourself.

Just recently Cathy was looking at some visuals of an 1814 re-enactor event at Longwoods (see note 1 below). Cathy doesn't normally channel, so she was taken by surprise when a spirit tried to contact her. Instead of a mind throttle; she got a psychic headache.

Cathy continues to receive paranormal feedback from her own drawings. Although she has tried, she hasn't been able to draw some pictures because the drawings themselves invoke strong reactions from the spirit world.

Cathy has experienced images from the spirit world on many occasions. The most significant image she continues to experience is a castle with Moorish designs, somewhere near water (*see note 2 below*). When Cathy was a child, she was able to draw magnificent Moorish designs from her *imagination*. She was unfamiliar with foreign concepts; yet, her art teacher was so impressed with her drawings that she showed the whole teaching staff. At the time, Cathy had no idea why the images were so popular with her teachers. Cathy has also experienced visions of Badajoz during the Napoleonic Wars, audible fife music and the spirit voices of British soldiers who had fought at Badajoz. In fact, everyone in our family has experienced audible fife music coming out of nowhere during the early morning hours.

* * *

Another incident occurred when both Cathy and Adam were viewing a poltergeist video recording on the internet. They weren't aware of the circumstances surrounding this particular poltergeist, but they both knew intuitively that this particular poltergeist was from the English civil war. After they made their comments out loud about the English civil war, they both received psychic headaches which hit both of them squarely in their "third eyes." Obviously, someone was trying to pass along something else with the poltergeist information. There was no harm done; however, the power rod cross was used to harmonize the room and eliminate the headaches. After everything had calmed down, Adam and Cathy did another search on the internet and found evidence that English civil war soldiers had indeed died in the basement of the same place where the poltergeist had been recorded.

Note (1): The Battle of Longwoods at Battle Hill took place near the Thames River where Tecumseh was defeated.

Note (2): We believe that Cathy's castle had something to do with Spain and the Napoleonic Wars.

Note (3): James Galloway settled in Ohio during the year 1797. He also became friends with Tecumseh. I was looking at James Galloway's cabin (of Greene County) on the internet. It felt like the front of my head was being pulled apart. The sensation was ten times more powerful than a highly charged crystal.

I had a problem keeping my hand on the computer mouse because both of my arms were vibrating. I received a similar jot from the Prophet's Town visuals (another Tecumseh attraction in Ohio); but my reaction wasn't nearly as potent. In both cases, I firmly believe that the energy surges were from my higher self.

Keeping the Home Fires Burning

Cathy went to visit Fort York with the boys for a few hours. She needed to pick up a custom chess piece for me which would replace the one that was taken from us in our previous home. The chess piece had been returned to us at our new home with some help from the spirit world; but it was taken again just after we moved in. I had a feeling that it would show up eventually; but I decided it would be easier to complete the set with another order.

On the day that Cathy and the boys visited the fort, there were only a few people in attendance. Nevertheless, whenever Cathy visits a fort with fewer people around, something always happens. This time an incident took place in the kitchen.

Cathy thought it was strange that there was a fire in the kitchen with no one attending to it. When she tried to open one of the kitchen doors, a spirit tried to stop her from leaving, by holding the door. At the same time, another door opened on its own.

Cathy arrived home later in the evening with the chess piece. The replacement chess piece was actually a British officer (a bishop) for my War of 1812 chess set. I placed "the bishop" with the rest of the chess pieces and stated my intentions. I claimed that the circle of protection was complete and that both sides of the chess set were now balanced. I asked that both armies should work together to protect our home against all unwanted entities. I did a patrol around the house with a couple of power rods. Then we all sat down and watched a few "Time Tunnel" episodes on DVD before we called it a day. I was on the verge of turning the gas fireplace off for the evening when Cathy stated that the smell coming from our family room was exactly the same as the Fort York fireplace. Because Cathy could smell burning wood from our gas fireplace, I was convinced that a sentry had been posted to our home and that he was making himself comfortable. More than likely he was also letting us know that he was on duty.

After I mentioned this, Cathy remarked, "I hope that the *Time Tunnel* program didn't frighten him too much."

I retrieved my tomahawk and a power rod and asked for extra energy, so I could transport the spirit back to the fort. I asked for "all Fort York soldiers" to form up in front of the chess set. I used some power rod techniques to transport the spirit (or spirits) back to Fort York.

After the ceremony was successfully completed, I told Cathy that it was possible that a soldier from the fort may have come back home with her. More than likely, the soldier made its presence known because of my request for protection; accordingly, when the soldier was sent back to the fort, the smell of burning wood went with him.

The Haunted War of 1812 Chess Set

I obtained the War of 1812 chess set because I was told that it would bring extra positive energy into our home (and we really did need the positive energy at the time). After I purchased the beautiful custom made set of American and British soldiers, I locked it up in a metal filing cabinet. It was going to be a birthday present for Adam. A few days later, Adam reported to me that there was a War of 1812 chess set sitting on my desk in my office. The interesting part was that the British and the Americans were facing off against each other. Moreover, the Americans appeared to be attacking the British (because the British had assumed a more defensive pose).

Adam channeled some information from the spirit world, so I could find out what was going on. He told me that the chess set didn't want to be locked up. If I locked it up again, the chess set would not help me at all.

The second item was that each side hated the other.

Given that I bought the chess set as protection for the house, I expected co-operation. After Adam said that each side hated the other, I said, "That would change."

As bizarre as this may be, one of the spirits assumed my son's form; and spoke directly to me in a disembodied voice. As the spokesperson for the chess set, he stated that all the spirits of the set would co-operate with each other in order to fight the evil in our home.

This is an update.

The Bishop (or the British officer as representative) had disappeared with a few of the soldiers while we were in our former home. I got everything back except the Bishop before we moved. After we moved, the Bishop showed up, but disappeared again shortly thereafter. I finally gave up and asked the artist who made the set to make me another Bishop. After living in our new home for approximately three years, we replaced the Bishop (see the previous entry Keeping the Home Fires Burning).

However, it was about four months *after* we acquired the replacement piece when Cathy asked me to observe the chess set. The chess set was in a cabinet which was located on a floor which tended to wobble. In other words, our 1812 chess set was never in perfect formation. However, today it was. The chess set was in perfect military formation, with the Americans on one side and the British on the other. They were all in a perfect line. Cathy said that it had taken time for the energy to come back to the set even though we had replaced the Bishop. (See note 1)

Four is the magic number and now the chess set had an overabundant amount of energy to spare. So what happens when you have an energy overload?

Later the same evening, the spirits played a classic prank on Adam. He was sitting on the floor watching television with his hand firmly around a full can of pop. Without warning, the can was taken from his hand. It kept going in front of him from side to side. He claimed that he couldn't figure how the spirit could keep the can from being taken back. Then, the grand finale: the can went straight up in the air about four feet off of the ground. The pop sprayed out like a sprinkler in a perfect circle and went all over him. Then the can came down in front of Adam without tipping over. Adam said that he thought that the can had been emptied; but when he checked there was still two thirds of the pop left over.

The strangest thing of all was that the pop was flat. There was not a bit of fizz left in it. Adam said that it tasted like it had been left open for a long time. This was one of the first stunts in our home which was more amusing than most and perhaps it was a result of someone having a bit of fun. Still, I gave them a taste of my power rod to teach them a lesson, so that it would not happen again.

Note: There was another reason why the chess set aligned itself which is explained in the next section.

Anniversary

It was the day after the chess set aligned itself. Cathy had been watching *Randall and Hopkirk* with the boys on DVD every night for the last three weeks. She picked up the R and H disc and was just about to put it in the machine when something made her change her mind. It was a sudden urge that made no sense. She walked over to a box of DVD-r discs which I had recorded several years ago. No one had seen the recordings other than myself. Out of the six discs, she chose Fort George. She later told me that intuitively she felt that she had no choice but to watch it.

After the film was shown, she went upstairs. About half way up to the second story landing, she could smell smoke. She asked Adam if he could smell the smoke as well. Cathy described the smell as burning wood which was different from the burning fireplace at Fort York. The area upstairs had also started to go cold. I strongly felt that the soldiers had used the "smell of smoke" as their calling card, so it was time to get into my 8th British Army redcoat. I also retrieved my two power rods just in case. I went around the house; then I went back to Cathy's upstairs office. I was on the verge of using the inverted power rods to transport the spirits when she claimed that someone had gently put their hand on her back and was trying very hard to communicate with her. At that point, I welcomed the soldiers to our home and I placed my own hand on her back. Everything settled down after that.

The following night, I decided to show the same DVD on Fort George to see what would happen. Adam claimed that when he made a few comments about the fort, everything went cold as before. After the show was over, Cathy went to her office. Instead of the smoke and the gentle hand; she got the same sad feelings which she always gets when she leaves the Niagara area where Fort George is situated.

It wasn't until the second showing of the DVD that we realized that the day before had been the anniversary of the Battle for Fort George. Wed. May 27th 2009 had been the 197th anniversary of the battle which resulted in Fort George being destroyed by American naval action. I strongly felt that the burning wood was not some warm-hearted message, but the actual burning of Fort George. I also believe that the anniversary burning which we experienced both cleansed and healed the soldier spirits who had experienced the battle 197 years before.

Note: Each chess piece continued to face forward in a perfect line, after the anniversary, in spite of the significant vibrations in the front room.

The Bully Ghost from 1812

The purpose of this selection is to illustrate how spirits can influence our behaviour.

Adam had a temper tantrum today. He was completely out of character. Cathy was making comments about how Adam was saying weird things with a British accent like "you may come in my room." I challenged Adam about being arrogant and short-tempered. He said that it was not possible either. He told me that just recently he was getting constant headaches. He finally admitted that the room which he loved so much was *becoming evil.* He tried to air it out and do a few other things; but within twelve hours, it was evil again.

I returned to his room with a large six inch obsidian pyramid, a double-headed Lemurian laser wand and my crystal power rod. I made my speech to the spirit invader about leaving our home. Making speeches is not particularly effective against evil spirits; but in our world, we seem to find it necessary. There is a remote possibility in some cases that an evil spirit will leave on its own.

Jacob came to the rescue with the full story. Apparently, the spirit was another stowaway from our old address. He was the spirit of a British soldier from the War of 1812. This one wasn't friendly either. From what I understood, the soldier was a bully, and he wanted to use Adam for that purpose. In other words, the spirit was only practicing what he knew when he was alive.

Adam's room was not protected at all. I didn't believe it was necessary because the house itself was protected. Because the spirit could not escape from Adam's room, it stayed in Adam's space and gained energy from Adam. Adam admitted later that his clock had moved around and there were a few other clues which he didn't take seriously at the time.

Now this spirit was powerful enough to evade my first attack; but Jacob was there and he could see him. Jacob fooled the spirit and captured him with my crystal power rod. Jacob then sent the spirit outside of our force field to the old elm tree. I asked Jacob to contact my guardian angel and the Council. We had the good spirits investigating our house, throughout the evening.

I put an eighteen-inch high, purple quartz crystal in Adam's room just to make sure. Things settled down in his room for a while; but our fight with evil spirits would continue.

The King's Flag

A shipment of re-enactor equipment had arrived from the United States in a large cardboard box which was approximately two feet wide by three feet tall. I left the box *unopened* in my office with the intent of checking it out later in the evening. However, that wasn't good enough for the spirits. Within half an hour, a large British flag was draped carefully over the box in a bold manner. I shall never forget the soldiers' display of love for their country's colours.

The Phantom Cat from 1812

Accordingly, to some sources of paranormal research, a phantom black cat has been seen in the basement of the White House over the past two hundred years. Apparently, the phantom cat likes to scare the hell out of anyone who is unfortunate to cross its path. Moreover, the phantom cat only appears when the United States is destined to become involved in a military adventure that will result in a high number of casualties.

I wrote about our phantom black cat in my previous book “Shadow People, 2009.” Our phantom black cat was with us in our previous home and has been seen by all of us on many separate occasions. I’ve seen him manifest himself, bump my mouse pad shelf, flash his furry black tail at me and disappear. I’ve also seen him manifest like a shadow and leap from a chair. In doing so, he knocked over some items, as if to prove that he really was there. On another occasion, I saw him in a semitransparent state, following me around in the basement. I could see right through him, thanks to the light from an overhead bulb which was in perfect position for the event. The phantom black cat got within six feet of me before he faded away in a striking ghostly fashion.

We consider our phantom black cat to be a family member and a constant companion because he has also been spotted around our current home. He appeared again during the fall of 2025 after being absent for a while. After mentioning the White House haunting to Cathy, I said to her, “Since a black phantom cat has been haunting the White House for the past two hundred years, wouldn't it be funny if our phantom cat was the culprit."

Issue of Spirit Pictures

Cathy asked me not to publish my "totem pole picture" of the spirit warriors taken at Fort Niagara because she strongly felt that the spirit soldiers wanted to prove their existence to me alone. There were several heads beside me and one hanging from the wall behind. It's a picture that you don't forget.

We have taken many pictures of semitransparent spirits from other places; but the one at Fort Niagara really blew me away because *the spooky faces looked rather solid.*

On the other hand, pictures can sometimes detract from the real issues. For starters, many people will assume that the pictures are fraudulent. If you don't believe in ghosts, pictures will hardly convince you otherwise. I've seen my own family come face to face with ghosts and still regard some of it as humbug. It takes more than a few knocks on the head to get a reaction (and knocks they got).

As mentioned elsewhere, I did publish the picture after the grinning jester face disappeared from over my left shoulder. The jester may not have been a soldier and that would had done the soldiers a disservice.

I also believe that enough time had passed and that it would be appropriate to publish the photo given the world situation we now live in. I thought that enough evidence might make some people think more deeply about our violent history and the paranormal.

Note: I published the original version of this book many years ago. While reviewing and re-editing the original manuscript, my only copy of the original paperback disappeared from my desk into the spirit world. At the same time Cathy had a nightmare related to the re-publication of the Haunted Forts and Battlefields of 1812. I've included it here because the nightmare happened right after I asked her which picture cover she thought was most appropriate for the new publication just before bedtime. There were soldier spirits going both ways from the Brock Monument on the front cover. With that on her mind, she told me the details of her nightmare. Her nightmare was about two large groups of people believing in something that wasn't true. Each group believed in the opposite of what they should have believed. Unfortunately, neither one was able to communicate with the other. Because Cathy was upset with the vision, she remembered it and told me about it; so I could share it with you. The nightmare was about the true path because I had a similar experience at Queenston Heights in my own visions. I've learned a great deal from the many energies that continue to exist from previous times. In keeping the balance, wisdom comes from learning from our past mistakes, rather than repeating them. When we balance the energies from the past, we discover the true path. The true path helps us to eliminate our fears.

The Old Fort Niagara Medallion

Cathy bought a beautiful souvenir at Fort Niagara a few years ago. On the front of the medallion read "OLD FORT NIAGARA" and "YOUNGSTOWN, NY." There was an image of the fort's gate and some marching British Redcoats on the medallion as well.

The back of the medallion was gold and the title read: "GATE OF THE FIVE NATIONS," followed by: "In 1755-1756, the French constructed a new gate in the land defenses of Fort Niagara and named it for the five nations of the Iroquois Confederacy."

Cathy had been using the medallion as a key chain for over two years, but she was getting worried that the back of the medallion would become worn. First of all, she put a flag of England on the key ring as a potential substitute. But as she was removing the medallion, she became dizzy and disoriented. It got worse until she finally put the medallion back on the key ring.

It was a cold day in early April, as I arrived back home from work. Cathy went to get her heavy coat from the clothes closet so that we could go for a walk together. A hat flew off the top shelf of the clothes closet. The crest of the British and American flags together, along with the words "Old Fort Niagara" were proudly displayed on the front of the cap. The flying baseball cap was given to us by the spirits as a symbolic gesture since we had not purchased or seen the hat before. We only know that British soldiers are still attached to the old fort and that the medallion is one of our links with them. Accordingly, we consider the cap to be just another friendly reminder of our role as guardians of the fort.

Bicentennial Map

I obtained several bicentennial maps which I wanted to laminate. Cathy took them to the shop and I fully expected to get the job done without a problem. She came back from the shop with a story instead. The first map jammed in the machine. The owner was panicking because it had never happened before. Moreover, he was looking at several thousand dollars worth of repairs if things didn't go well. Fortunately, they were able to correct the problem and save the first map.

The bicentennial map told the story of the War of 1812. I saw the small tear on the one corner and it looked like a few long wrinkle marks on one side of the map. I didn't check the other side until a month later. When I finally did check the other side of the map, there was less damage to the print; but I was amazed to see a white mark go from Lake Ontario towards Fort Niagara and down the Niagara River. The white line actually separated Fort Niagara from Fort George. Because the mark was only on one small section of the map and was in reference to Fort George and Fort Niagara, I would say that the whole incident was deliberate.

Afterword

I consider my knowledge of the spirits at Fort George to be personal. But I will volunteer the following information:

- The spirits at Fort George are as real to me as any human being. Many people who work at the fort through Parks Canada, either as full time or as summer students have probably felt their presence.

- Because of the bicentennial, there were many changes to the fort. The palisade, the roofing and many other changes created a problem with the energies and something had to be done about it. Let's just say that I helped the soldiers.

- The soldiers also have views on the re-enactments at the fort. They appear to like the scouts' annual re-enactment in September which my two boys and I have been involved with for many years.

- However, there were some mixed reactions to some of the other re-enactments which tend to be more realistic.

The following applies *to all the haunted forts and battlefields* we have visited:

- We have experienced intense negativity after visiting Fort Mississauga and Chippewa. Accordingly, it's not unusual to feel uncomfortable or "not welcomed" when you're dealing with pockets of "mixed energies," related to different layers of the past.

- If you feel uncomfortable with the spirits because you can't see them, you can still harmonize with them by balancing your energy with the forts while visiting. In general, the forts are more forgiving then battlefields and war memorials, if you are sensitive to psychic phenomena.

A word of warning: Do not assume that you know the best interests of the fort's spirits if you are psychic. Being psychic will not impress them. In fact, there a good chance that you will pick up some negative feedback from previous times instead which I understand has the potential to make people sick to their stomachs.

Appendix I

Cycle of War

(Limited Beliefs vs. Awareness)

Peace

War + **Anger**

Aggression

Note: Anger is related to negativity which leads to aggression. Aggression along with anger can lead to war. Once balance returns to the cycle of anger, aggression and war there is a return to peace.

Contributors: The Fathers of Fort George

Appendix II

Cycle of Negativity

(Limited Beliefs vs. Awareness)

Balance

Protection + **Negativity**

Imbalance

Note: Negativity is part of our world. We don't need to judge it. We just need to counter it with positive strategies to keep things in balance.

Appendix III

Cycle of Negative Energy Imbalances (Spirit World)

(Limited Beliefs vs. Awareness)

Balance

Shared Energies + **Negativity**

Imbalance

Note: Negativity created by mixed energies creates an imbalance in both the material world and the spirit world. Harmonized shared energies promotes both healing and enlightenment. Therefore, humans have a role to play in keeping negativity in balance in the spirit world. Shakespeare's Midsummer Night's Dream was more about truth than most people realize.

Bibliography

Berton, P. The Invasion of Canada 1812-1813. Toronto: McClelland and Steward Ltd., 1980.

Berton, P. Flames across the Border 1813-1814. Toronto: McClelland and Steward Ltd., 1981.

Hook, J. Tecumseh: Visionary Chief of the Shawnee. Poole, Dorset: Firebird Books Ltd., 1980.

Jourdain, E. and Moberly, A. An Adventure. London: Faber and Faber Ltd., 1911.

Shooting Star, C.T. Shadow People: A Journal of the Paranormal. Bloomington, IN: iuniverse Publishing, 2009.

Shooting Star, C.T. Shadow Moon: The Wisdom of the Light Fortress and its Opponents. Victoria, B.C.: First Choice Books Publishing, 2021.

Steiger, B. Real Ghosts, Restless Spirits and Haunted Places. Canton, MI: Visible Ink Press, 2003.

Upton, K. Ghosts of Niagara 2. Self-published, 2004.

www.ingramcontent.com/pod-product-compliance
Lightning Source LLC
LaVergne TN
LVHW050644100826
845148LV00011B/1978

* 9 7 9 8 9 5 0 0 7 2 1 2 3 *